Language Tree

Student's Book 3

Second Edition

macmillan education

Macmillan Education
4 Crinan Street
London, N1 9XW
A division of Springer Nature Limited

Companies and representatives throughout the world

www.macmillan-caribbean.com

ISBN 978-0-230-48145-9

This edition published 2016
First edition published 2006

Designed by Macmillan Education and Blue Dog Design Studio
Illustrated by Jan Smith c/o Beehive; Pamela Goodchild c/o B.L. Kearley; Anni Axworthy, Dave Hill, Bethan Matthews and Lisa Williams c/o Sylvie Poggio
Cover design by Macmillan Education and Clare Webber
Cover illustration by Nathalie Gavet
Typeset by Tek-Art

The author and publishers would like to thank the following education professionals for their valuable contributions to this edition:
Suzette Abbott-King (*St Vincent*), Leonie Alexander-Charles (*St Vincent*), Ingrid Daniel-Simon (*Antigua*), Janelle Little (*Barbados*), Tessa McQuilkin (*Grenada*), Christina Morris (*Barbados*), Rochelle Richards (*Antigua*), Edwina Riviere (*Dominica*), Carla St. Louis (*Grenada*) and Sandra Thomas (*Grenada*)

The authors and publishers would like to thank the following for permission to reproduce their photographs:
Alamy/foodfolio p54, Alamy/frans lemmens p93(tr), Alamy/Dawna Moore p89, Alamy/National Geographic Image Collection pp4(cr), 88, Alamy/M. Timothy O'Keefe p124(bl), Alamy/Prisma Bildagentur AG p93(tl), Alamy/Rolf Richardson p55, Alamy/Julian Worker p95: **Corbis**/Cultura/Camarena p43; **Getty Images**/Murray Cooper p125, Getty Images/Ryan McVay pp4(bm), 96, Getty Images/Mint Images - Frans Lanting p91(tr), Getty Images/Tetra images p124(tr); **Joseph Jones** p84; **Thinkstock**/Design Pics p91(br), Thinkstock/iStock/whammer121736 p93(tm).

The author and publisher are grateful for permission to reproduce the following copyright material:
Steel Band Jump © 1994 Faustin Charles. From A CARIBBEAN DOZEN edited by John Agard & Grace Nichols. Reproduced by permission of Walker Books Ltd, London SE11 5HJ www.walker.co.uk
Poem: *Drinking Water – Coconut* by Grace Nichols. Reproduced with permission of Curtis Brown Group Ltd, London on behalf of Grace Nichols. Copyright © Grace Nichols 1988.

Printed and bound in Italy by L.E.G.O. S.p.A. Lavis (TN)

2019
10 9 8

Contents

How to Use this Book

Language Tree Level 3 follows an integrated approach, and language skills in each unit develop naturally out of the reading text. Use the Student's Book alongside the Workbook and online Teacher's Resources (www.bit.ly/LangTree2e) to develop and practise important reading, listening, speaking and comprehension skills.

Teaching units

There are 18 teaching units, each comprising the following sections:

Get ready

This section gives ideas for a class discussion which introduces the reading passage and draws on the students' experience. It also draws attention to the type of text (fiction, non-fiction etc.) and introduces key vocabulary.

Reading

The passages cover a variety of text types. Students can read independently or take it in turn to read a section. Encourage students to work out the meaning of unfamiliar vocabulary from the context.

Comprehension questions require students to recall detail, make inferences, draw conclusions, identify cause and effect, express personal opinions and note the differences between different text types. Questions can be tackled orally or in writing, depending on the needs of the class. It may be appropriate to talk through the questions before asking students to write answers to some of them.

Unit 13 Turtles

Get ready

What do you know about turtles?
What would you like to find out about them?

K	W	L
What I know	What I want to know	What I learned

Reading

The Leatherback Sea Turtle

Leatherback sea turtles have lived in our oceans for 65 million years. They are the largest living turtles. They can be up to two metres long and often weigh more than 300 kilograms. They eat jellyfish and sea plants. They often live more than 40 years.

Where Leatherbacks Live

Leatherbacks spend almost all their life in the sea. However, females always return to the beach where they hatched to lay their eggs. They nest on beaches in the West Indies, in South America and in West Africa.

88

- Get ready: Draw the **KWL chart** on the board. Discuss with students and fill the first two columns with their suggestions. You will complete the third column after reading.
- Pre-reading: Get students to **survey** the text by looking at the layout, photos and headings. Ask: *What kind of text is it (fiction / fact)? What kind of information will you find in it?*

Speaking and listening: discuss an issue

1. **What kind of waste can be recycled? Make two lists:**
   - Things we use at home which can be recycled.
   - Things we use at school which can be recycled.
2. **How do you think we could create less waste?**

Speaking and listening

This symbol before these exercises indicates that students work with a partner. Exercises include discussion, planning and role play. Move around the class, checking on progress, or work alongside students who find oral work challenging.

Language work

Teaching points are followed by practice exercises. Work through the example together before asking students to work on an Exercise. Some students can write their answers independently or in pairs. You may need to work orally with other students, writing the answers on a large sheet of paper which they can all see.

> **Language: prepositions**
>
> **Prepositions** are words which tell us *where* people or things are.
> *Greg went into the yard.*
> *Into* tells us where Greg went.

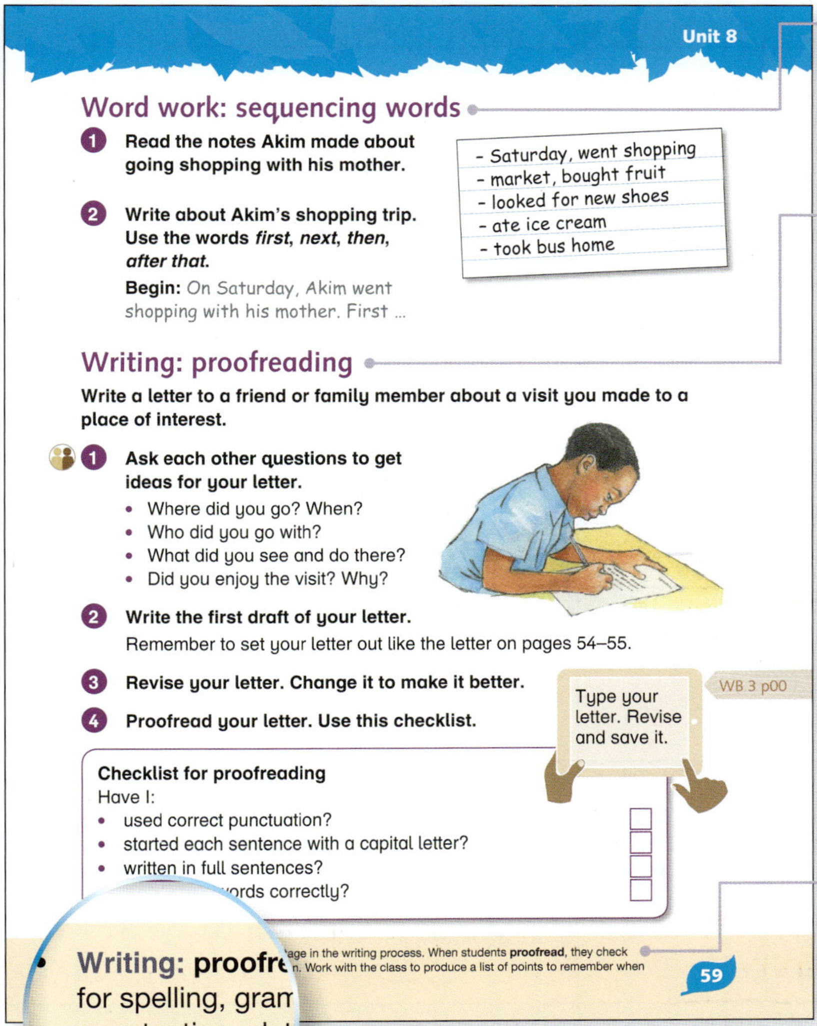

Unit 8

Word work: sequencing words

1 **Read the notes Akim made about going shopping with his mother.**

- Saturday, went shopping
- market, bought fruit
- looked for new shoes
- ate ice cream
- took bus home

2 **Write about Akim's shopping trip. Use the words *first*, *next*, *then*, *after that*.**

Begin: On Saturday, Akim went shopping with his mother. First …

Writing: proofreading

Write a letter to a friend or family member about a visit you made to a place of interest.

1 **Ask each other questions to get ideas for your letter.**
- Where did you go? When?
- Who did you go with?
- What did you see and do there?
- Did you enjoy the visit? Why?

2 **Write the first draft of your letter.**
Remember to set your letter out like the letter on pages 54–55.

3 **Revise your letter. Change it to make it better.**

4 **Proofread your letter. Use this checklist.**

Type your letter. Revise and save it.

WB 3 p00

Checklist for proofreading
Have I:
- used correct punctuation?
- started each sentence with a capital letter?
- written in full sentences?
- …ords correctly?

…age in the writing process. When students **proofread**, they check …n. Work with the class to produce a list of points to remember when

59

Word work

Examples of word-level work, such as vocabulary, prefixes or homophones are drawn from the reading passage wherever possible.

Writing

See page 128 for an overview of the writing process which underpins all the writing exercises in *Language Tree*.

The first stage – getting ideas – is very important. It provides the material for students to work with. If students miss out this stage they are likely to say, "I don't know what to write." You may begin work as a class – brainstorming ideas and useful vocabulary on the board.

Some students will be able to complete the writing task on their own or in mixed ability pairs. You may need to support other students by working alongside them, writing a group composition for which you act as a scribe. Encourage students to check and revise their work.

This feature supports integrating technology into students' learning.

On-the-page teacher's notes

There are suggestions for introducing and extending the exercises at the bottom of each page.

DA This symbol precedes suggestions for working with students of different abilities.

To help with planning, syllabus objectives are highlighted in bold type.

WB 3 p10 indicates that a skill is further practised in the Workbook.

Looking Back

Skills are revisited in three 'Looking Back' sections. Use the exercises to assess in which areas students need further support.

Scope and Sequence chart and Skills Index

These sections will support your short- and long-term planning, enabling you to make sure that you are covering the syllabus.

Scope and Sequence

Reading	Reading and comprehension	Speaking and listening
1 *The Swing*	• Predict story • Revise predictions	Retell story: beginning, middle, end
2 *A Special Visitor*	• Recall details • Question and answer relationships	• Generate questions to elicit information • Role play an interview
3 *Going to the Library*	Predict content from picture	Distinguish between fiction and non-fiction
4 *Tortoise Tries to Fly*	• Describe character • Discuss 'lesson' of story	Discuss how to complete a story plan
5 *Clean-up Day*	• Inferring • Problem solving	Discuss problem and plan a solution
6 *Steel Band Jump Up*	Features of poems: rhymes, repetition, rhythm	• Recite a poem • Peer evaluation
Looking Back 1	• Predict story • Question and answer relationships	
7 *Anansi Stories*	Draw inferences from pictures	Discuss character in stories
8 *The Class Visit*	• Study letter format • Answer inferential questions	Question and answer about visit to place of interest
9 *Drinking Water-Coconut*	• Notice the layout of a poem • Identify rhyming words	Discuss appeal to senses
10 *Exciting News*	• Skim for general idea • Identify relevant information	Role play planning a trip
11 *Read the Label!*	• Distinguish between fact and opinion • Identify audience and purpose	Evaluate content and presentation
12 *All's Well That Ends Well*	• Make predictions • Discuss behaviour	Use a street plan to give directions
Looking Back 2	Letter format	
13 *Turtles*	Use prior knowledge (KWL chart)	Discuss information sources
14 *The Three R's*	• Identify main idea and supporting detail • Use a glossary	• Discuss an issue • Express opinion
15 *The Speech*	• Give and justify opinion • Make notes	• Prepare and give a short speech • Peer evaluation
16 *Grace Goes to School*	• Identify narrator • Understand cause and effect	Discuss how to solve a problem
17 *The Water Cycle*	Interpret diagrams	• Study skills • Interpret graphical material
18 *The Missing Cake*	Identify features of a play	• Act a scene from a play • Create a new scene
Looking Back 3	• Use a glossary • Recall details	

Language	Word work	Writing
• Nouns: proper, common • Noun plurals	Irregular plurals	Pre-writing: • getting ideas • write new story ending
Present tense: • subject–verb agreement • *am, is, are* • *have, has*	Words in context	Ask and answer personal questions
Present tense: • negative, questions • verb endings: *-tch*, *-sh*, *-x*	• Dictionary skills • Alphabetical order	Write personal information for an application form
• Sentences • Sentence punctuation	Collective nouns	Pre-writing: • planning • use story plan to plan own story
Pronouns: subject and object	Synonyms	Drafting: draft and revise report
• Present continuous • Present participle	Features of poems: similes, onomatopoeia	Write a name poem
Revise: present tense, plural nouns, sentences, pronouns, present continuous	Context	Write a report of event
• Simple past tense • Regular and irregular verbs	Root words	• Describe a story character • Revising
• Past tense: - interrogative and negative - *was, were* • Commas in letters	Sequencing words	• Write a friendly letter giving account of event • Proofreading
• Adjectives: identify • Comparative and superlative	Suffixes: *-y*, *-ful*, *-less*	Write sensory description
• Simple future tense • Possessives: *my*, *mine*, etc.	Syllables	Write text of email
• Articles: - *the, a, an* - *some, any* • Abbreviations	Spelling tips	Design an advertisement
Prepositions	Prefixes: *dis-*, *un-*, *im-*	• Write your own story • Use whole writing process • Publishing
Revise: possessives, past tense, comparative and superlative adjectives	• Syllables • Root words	Write letter of invitation
Adverbs	Use index and table of contents	• Record information in a table • Write sentences
• Conjunctions: *and, but, because* • Commas in lists	Prefix: *re-*	Write a paragraph: • main idea • supporting detail
Apostrophes: • possessive nouns • contractions: *its, it's*	Opposites	Write short speech
Quotation marks	Homophones	Plan and write a story about a problem
Instructions	Compound nouns	Write about information presented graphically
• Conjunctions: *while, before, after* • Relative pronouns: *who, which*	Homographs	Write a scene for a play
Revise: adverbs, conjunctions, quotation marks, possessive nouns	Opposites	• Prepare fact sheet • Write expository paragraph

Unit 1 The Swing

Get ready

What kind of games do you play when you are outside?
What do you do when you can't play outside?

Reading

The Swing

There were a lot of trees outside Andrew and Javon's house. Their father tied a rope to a branch of a big breadfruit tree. The boys loved swinging on it.

Last September there was a big storm. Andrew and Javon could not play outside for two days. Then the sun began to shine again.

"You can play in the garden today," Daddy told the boys, "but don't swing on the rope. It could be dangerous."

The boys ran outside. They kicked a ball and they ran races.

"Let's swing on the rope," said Javon.

"Daddy told us not to," said Andrew.

"We won't go very high," said Javon.

The boys swung backwards and forwards on the rope. They went faster and faster. They did not see that the neighbour, Mrs. Roberts, was watching them.

- **Get ready:** This section introduces the theme of the unit. Help students to draw on **prior experience** to prepare for the reading exercise.
- Pre-reading: Tell students to look for clues in the pictures and **predict** what they think the story is about. Half-way through the story ask them if they want to change anything in their predictions. At the end of the story, **review their predictions** and discuss what may have been different in the story.

HW

Suddenly, there was a loud crack. The boys fell on the ground and a branch fell on top of them. They ran back into the house.

In the afternoon Daddy came home. He stopped to talk to Mrs. Roberts. Then he came into the house.

"Come here, boys," he commanded. "Did you swing on the rope?"

"No, Daddy," said Javon. "A big monkey came into the garden. It swung on the rope and the branch broke."

"Boys, you know that is not true. Mrs. Roberts saw you."

The boys were ashamed. "We are very sorry, Daddy," they whispered.

1 Who made a swing for the boys? — *Right there*

2 How long did the boys stay inside when it rained?

3 What happened when they swung on the rope?

4 Who saw what the boys did?

5 How did Daddy know that the boys were not telling the truth? — *Think and search*

6 The boys were *ashamed*. What does this mean?

   a) They were afraid because Daddy was vexed.

   b) They thought they would get into trouble.

   c) They knew they had done something wrong.

7 What lesson can be learnt from this story? — *On your own*

8 What do you think Daddy should do next? Why?

- Comprehension: Remind students of **question-answer relationships (QAR)**. For questions 1–4, answers can be found **right there** in the text. For questions 5 and 6, students can find the answers in the text, but they must **think and search** to find them. Questions 7 and 8 require students to use **their own ideas**, based on what they have read in the text.

DA Students can write answers to questions 1–6 according to ability. Give all students the chance to discuss the answers to questions 7 and 8.
NOTE: *In these teacher's notes, whenever you see this icon* DA *there will be suggestions for working with students of different abilities.*

Story structure

Stories must have a **beginning**, a **middle** and an **end**.

Beginning	**Middle**	**End**
Introduces the characters. Tells us what the story is about.	Tells us what the characters do and what problems they have.	Sorts out problems. Tells us how things finish and the lesson learnt.

Speaking and listening

Retell the story of 'The Swing'.

- What happened at the beginning of the story?
- What happened in the middle?
- What happened at the end?

Language

Nouns

Nouns name things, people, animals and places. These words are **common nouns**: *swing* *neighbour* *monkey* *garden*

WB 3 p29

1 **List four common nouns under each heading.**

things	people	animals	places
rope	family	dog	market

2 **Find six different nouns in this story.**

Example: sister

My little sister is very greedy. She loves eating cakes and sweets. Once, my mother baked a chocolate cake. She left it in the kitchen. My sister found the cake and took a big slice. When my mother found her, her face was covered in chocolate.

- **Speaking and listening:** Prepare for the exercise by brainstorming the events in 'The Swing'. Then get students to put the events in **sequence**.

Proper nouns

The names of people or places, the days of the week and the months of the year are **proper nouns**. They begin with capital letters.

Daddy *Antigua* *March* *Friday*

3 **Find five proper nouns in the story 'The Swing'.** WB 3 p29

4 **Write the sentences. Use capital letters for the proper nouns.**

1 There was a big storm on friday.
2 My mother's birthday is in march.
3 andrew and javon like playing in the garden.
4 mrs. roberts saw the boys on the swing.
5 My friend jaydon lives in kingstown.
6 ricardo went to bridgetown on saturday.

5 **Answer the questions. Use capital letters for the proper nouns.**

1 When is your birthday?
2 What is your mother's name?
3 What day is it tomorrow?
4 Where do you live?

Singular and plural nouns

Singular means one. **Plural** means more than one.
We add 's' to most nouns to make them plural.

tree ➔ *trees* *rope* ➔ *ropes*

6 **Read the story. Find the singular and plural nouns.**

Jordan often plays with his brother in the garden. They run races and chase their dog. Daddy sometimes plays football with them. If it rains, the boys go into the house and play with their toys. Mommy makes delicious snacks for them to eat.

Write two lists.

Singular nouns: Jordan Plural nouns: races

DA Exercise 4: Questions 5 and 6 are more challenging.
DA Exercise 5: Encourage students to answer in complete sentences, but allow some students to answer with one word, according to ability.

For nouns ending in 's', 'sh', 'tch' or 'x' we add '**es**': bus ➔ bus**es**
For most nouns ending in 'o' add '**es**': tomato ➔ tomato**es**
For nouns ending in 'y' change 'y' to '**i**' and add '**es**': baby ➔ bab**ies**
For nouns ending in 'f' change 'f' to '**v**' and add '**es**': leaf ➔ lea**ves**

7 **Write the correct plural nouns.**

a bus	three buses	a brush	two brushes
a glass	four glasses	a box	five boxes
a branch	six branches	a patch	two patches
a loaf	two loaves	a wife	three wives
a cherry	ten cherries	a fly	ten flies

WB 3 p32 **8** **Choose nouns from the list below to complete the poem. Write their plurals in the spaces.**

tomato leaf wife match branch
mango knife potato patch

My Crazy Dream
I dreamt I saw some flowers with leaves,
A cook with potatoes, men and their wives.
Then I saw a dress with patches,
A tree with branches, a box of matches.
Next I saw some red knives,
Juicy tomatoes and sweet mangoes.

9 **Write the plurals of these nouns.**

day *monkey*
boy *story* *toy*
country *key*

Remember!
Nouns ending in 'ay', 'ey', 'oy' add '**s**' in the plural.
donkey ➔ *donkeys*
day ➔ *days*

- Plurals in 'es': Help students to create their own **mnemonics** to help them remember the rule about adding 'es' to plural nouns, e.g. a series of words: *bus, box, wash, watch*.
- Extension: Some students can write an extra verse for the poem using plural nouns.

Word work: irregular plurals

1 **Match the nouns in the circles.**

Example: man – men

~~man~~
child woman foot
tooth mouse

women
feet ~~men~~ mice
children teeth

Remember!
Some nouns have special plurals:
child ➔ *children*

WB 3 p33

2 **Write down the pairs and learn how to spell the plurals.**

3 **Choose three of the plural nouns. Use them in your own sentences.**

Example: The children love eating ice cream.

Writing: write a new story ending

Getting ideas

1 **Discuss what happens next in the story about the swing.**

I think the boys had to stay inside.

I think Daddy mended the swing for them.

2 **Write your own new story ending.**

3 **Read your story ending to another student.**

Ask this student to tell you:

- what he or she liked about your ending.
- how you could make your story ending better.

- **Word work:** Remind students that some plural nouns have special spellings, e.g. **man – men**.
- You may wish to tell students that special plurals are **irregular** plurals.
- **Writing: Pre-writing** is an important stage in the writing process. Help your students **get ideas** for their new story ending by discussing what they can see in the picture. They can discuss whether Daddy should mend the swing or not. Allow them to express their opinions freely.

Unit 2 A Special Visitor

Get ready

Which famous person would you like to meet?
What questions would you like to ask this person?

Reading

A Special Visitor

Mr. Brown: Good morning everyone. We have a special visitor today, Chantelle Jackson. Please welcome her.

Chantelle: Thank you, Mr. Brown. I'm happy to be here.

Mr. Brown: Ten years ago, Chantelle was in my class. Now she is famous.

Chantelle: I am not famous yet, Mr. Brown.

Mr. Brown: You soon will be. Please tell us what you do.

Chantelle: I am a swimmer. I compete in swimming races.

Mr. Brown: Who would like to ask Chantelle a question?

Sam: I would. Which was your best race?

Chantelle: I won a gold medal in the 100 metre Junior Swimming Championship last year.

Emma: Why did you become a swimmer?

Chantelle: My father taught me to swim when I was very small. I have always loved swimming. I train every day.

Shane: How long do you train each day?

Chantelle: About three hours. It is difficult because I have to study as well.

- **Get ready:** Help students to draw on **prior experience** to prepare for the reading exercise.
- Before reading: Draw attention to the layout of the reading text. Point out that the names on the left indicate who is speaking.
- Students can **predict** the content of the reading text by drawing **inferences** from the picture. Ask: *Who do you think the people are? What is the young woman wearing around her neck?*

Emma: Where do you live now?
Chantelle: I go to college in the USA but I come back to St. Vincent when I can to see my family.
Sam: What do you eat?
Emma: You always want to know about food, Sam.
Chantelle: No, that's a good question. I eat a lot of bread, rice and potatoes. They give me energy. I do not eat sweets.
Mr. Brown: Thank you, Chantelle. Now, if you have time, come and watch us play football.

Right there

1 When was Chantelle in Mr. Brown's class?
2 What does she do now?
3 Why was the 100 metre race Chantelle's best race?
4 Why is it difficult for Chantelle to train?
5 What two things does Chantelle do to help her perform well?

Think and search

6 Why has Chantelle come back to her old school?
   a) To see her old school friends.
   b) To talk to the students about her sport.
   c) To watch the students play football.

On your own

7 Which sports do you like? Do you prefer to watch them or to play them?
8 Would you like to become a famous sportsman or sportswoman? Why? Why not?

- Comprehension: Discuss with students where they can find the answers to the comprehension questions. The questions can be answered orally or in writing according to the needs of your students.

DA Students can write answers to questions 1–6 according to ability. Give all students the chance to discuss the answers to questions 7 and 8.

Speaking and listening: asking questions

1 Find questions in the conversation which begin with these words.

Why? | Where? | Which? | What? | How?

2 Role play an interview with a famous person.

- Choose a famous person.
- Make a list of questions to ask this person.
- One of you plays the role of the famous person.
- The other asks this person questions.

Language: present tense

Verbs are words which tell us what people do.

*I **train** every day.*

Train is a verb. It tells us what Chantelle does.

1 Find the verbs in these sentences.

1. I go to college in the USA.
2. Chantelle competes in swimming races.
3. Chantelle's family lives in St. Vincent.
4. She eats a lot of bread, rice and potatoes.
5. They give her energy.
6. The students ask Chantelle a lot of questions.

- **Speaking and listening:** Help students to **generate questions** to elicit information. Move around the class while your students prepare the role play to give help where needed. Invite some pairs to perform their role plays to the class.
- **Language:** Go through the exercises orally first.

DA Allow students to answer some or all the questions according to ability.

The **present tense** can tell us what usually or currently happens.

I *play* football on Friday.

We add 's' to the present tense verb when we talk about *one* person, animal or thing.

Ben *plays* football on Friday.

On Saturday he *helps* at home.

2 Choose the correct verb forms.

1 Sheena (*think / thinks*) about food all the time.
2 Sam and Emma (*ask / asks*) questions.
3 I (*walk / walks*) to school in the morning.
4 My father (*work / works*) in the town.
5 We (*like / likes*) sports.
6 Jason (*train / trains*) on Saturdays.

3 Make six sentences. Remember to use the correct form of the verb. WB 3 p47

Example: My friends like reading.

1 My friends 2 Mr. Brown 3 We 4 My mother 5 I 6 She	like likes	swimming. music. going to the beach. reading. playing cricket. climbing trees.

4 Choose verbs from the box to complete the story.

begin get write play read love walk

John __gets__ up early in the morning. He ________ school with his friends. School ________ at 8 o'clock. The children ________ books and ________ stories. After school John ________ football with his friends. They all ________ football.

Remember!
You will need to add '**s**' to some of the verbs.

- Exercise 2, Subject–verb agreement: Remind students that only verbs in the 3rd person singular (*he, she, it*) add 's' in the present tense. Explain that Ben in the example follows the same rule as 'he'. 'Sam and Emma follow the same rule as 'they'.
- Exercise 3: If appropriate, you may wish to introduce **subject** and **predicate** here. Tell your students that the subject (in the left column of the table) performs the action. The rest of the sentence (containing the verb) is the predicate.

Remember the special forms **am**, **is** and **are**.
*I **am** a swimmer. She **is** famous. Sam and Emma **are** in Mr. Brown's class.*

WB 3 p51

5 **Copy and complete the sentences with *am*, *is* or *are*.**

1. Chantelle __is__ a swimming champion.
2. I ________ on the school football team.
3. We ________ good at sports.
4. It ________ hard to train for three hours.
5. Terry and Dwayne ________ not at school today.
6. Some races ________ very long.

Have or **has?** Study the examples.
*I **have** a bicycle. My brother **has** a car.*
*My parents **have** a big house.*

WB 3 p51

6 **Complete the sentences with *have* or *has*.**

1. I __have__ some new football boots.
2. The students ________ a visitor today.
3. Shane ________ two brothers.
4. You ________ my book.
5. My sister and I ________ a new puppy.
6. Our puppy ________ black and white spots.

7 **Make sentences about yourself and other people.**

Example: My teacher is kind. She has a red car.

- I am ____________. I have ____________.
- My brother/sister is ____________. He/she has ______________.
- My friends are ____________. They have ____________.

- Am, is / are, have / has: You may find it helpful to write the verbs out for students to see: e.g. *I am, you are, he/she/it is, we/they are*.
- Exercise 7: Practise making sentences with the whole class before students write.
- Extension: Students can make sentences about several family members.

Word work: context

Look for **clues** to help you understand new words.
You can find clues in the **context** (the words and sentences around).

*Chantelle **competes** in swimming races.*

Competes means 'takes part in competitions'. The clue is in the rest of the sentence.

What do the underlined words mean?

WB 3 p96

1 One day Chantelle will win a lot of medals and become famous.
a) old **b)** well-known **c)** unhappy

2 The students were fascinated to hear about Chantelle's gold medal.
a) interested **b)** bored **c)** scared

3 Sportsmen and women need to train frequently to keep fit.
a) sometimes **b)** often **c)** not very often

4 Sportsmen and women need to eat a diet which gives energy.
a) training **b)** clothes **c)** food

Writing: dialogue

1 **Match the questions and answers.**

When did you start playing cricket?	My sports teacher.
Who taught you to play cricket?	I live in Barbados.
Where do you live now?	I started playing at school.

2 **Write your own interview.**

Use the questions and answers you prepared in the 'Speaking and listening exercise', or write a new interview.

- **Writing:** Lead in to the writing exercise by asking students to suggest their own questions.
- Exercise 2: Ask some student pairs to perform their role plays again. Write one of the role plays on the board as an example. Remind students to set out their interviews like the interview in the reading passage on pages 14–15.

DA Some students may write only one question and answer in Exercises 1 and 2.

Unit 3 Going to the Library

Get ready

What kind of books do you enjoy reading most? Why?
Where would you go to find out information?

Reading

Going to the Library

Kayla and Joshua love reading. Every week their mother takes them to the public library. There is a children's section in the library where Kayla and Joshua can choose books to take home.

Last week Joshua saw his friend Daniel in the library. "Hello, Daniel," he said quietly. "Do you often come to the library?"

"No, this is my first visit," Daniel said.

"Would you like me to show you around?" Joshua offered.

First the boys went to the fiction section of the library. "This is where you find story books, plays and poems," Joshua told his friend.

Then they went to the reference section. "This is where you go to find out information," said Joshua.

"Do you enjoy coming to the library?" asked Daniel.

"Oh yes! I love Mrs. Webster's library club," Joshua answered.

- **Get ready:** Get students to discuss their reading preferences and to suggest different sources of information, e.g. *parents, teachers, books, encyclopaedias, internet*.
- **Reading:** To prepare for the reading exercise ask students to use the pictures to predict what the text will be about. Ask questions, e.g. *Where are the children? What are they doing there?*

“Does Mrs. Webster read you stories?”

“Yes, she does. Sometimes she helps us use the computers to look up things on the internet.”

“I’d like to go to the library club,” said Daniel. “How do I join the library?”

“You must ask the librarian for a form for your mother to sign. Then you can take books out.”

“Do I have to pay?” asked Daniel.

“No,” replied Joshua. “You don’t need to pay. You only pay if you don’t return the books on time.”

1 Who takes Kayla and Joshua to the library?

2 Why does Joshua offer to show Daniel around the library?

3 In which section of the library can you find story books?

4 Where do you go to find out information?

5 How much does it cost to borrow books from the library?

6 Who is a librarian?

a) A person who borrows books from a library.

b) A person who uses the computers in a library.

c) A person who looks after the books in a library.

7 Why is it important to be quiet in a library?

8 Do you think going to the library is important? Why?

- Comprehension: For questions 1–4, answers can be found *right there* in the text. For questions 5 and 6, students must *think* and *search* for the answers. Questions 7 and 8 are *on your own* questions where students give their own answers, based on what they know about libraries.

DA Allow students to write answers to fewer questions, according to their ability.

Speaking and listening: fiction and non-fiction

Stories tell us about things which are not real. They are **fiction**. Information books tell us about real things. They tell us **facts**. They are **non-fiction**.

Ask and answer with a partner.

- Which of the following books are fiction?
- Which are non-fiction?

WB 3 p94

stories	science books	poems	encyclopaedias
plays	travel books	cook books	sports books

Language

Present tense

We use **do** or **does** to ask questions in the present tense.
Do *you* ***enjoy*** *coming to the library?*
Does *Mrs. Webster* ***read*** *you stories?*
Where ***do*** *Kayla and Joshua* ***go*** *every week?*

1 Complete the questions.

Example: Do *you take books out of the library?*

1 ________ your teacher often tell you stories?
2 ________ Kayla and Joshua like going to the library?
3 Which story character ________ you like?
4 Where ________ you go on Saturdays?
5 ________ your mother take you shopping?
6 Where ________ your grandmother live?

2 Make up three questions to ask your partner.

Do you like reading stories?

- **Speaking and listening:** Give students examples of book titles to help them distinguish between fiction and non-fiction, e.g. *Tales of Anansi, How to Play Chess*.
- **Language,** Subject–verb agreement: Remind students to use *does* with the 3rd person singular (e.g. *Joshua, he, she, it*).

3 Write questions in the present tense.

WB 3 p49

Example: Which stories do you like?

1 Which stories / you like?
2 When / Joshua go to the library?
3 What / Kayla do on Sundays?
4 Where / a librarian work?
5 How / you play marbles?
6 What / Joel eat for lunch?

We also use **do** or **does** with negative sentences.
*You **do not need** to pay.*
*Daniel **does not go** to the library club.*

4 Write negative sentences.

WB 3 p50

Example: *The girls* do not *go to school on Saturday.*

The girls We Kayla I Daniel	does not do not	go to school on Saturday. pay to join the library. like stories with a sad ending. love going to the library. know how to find a book.

5 Write about what Kim does on Saturdays.

Example: She does not stay at home. She visits Grandma.

1 stay at home ✗
2 visit Grandma ✓
3 help to cook lunch ✓
4 see her friends ✗
5 read stories ✓
6 play in the garden ✓
7 go shopping ✗
8 do homework ✗

6 Write about what you do on Saturdays.

- Write two sentences saying what you do.
- Write two sentences saying what you do *not* do.

- Exercise 5: The options followed by '✗' indicate what Kim does NOT do. Remind students that we add 's' to verbs when we talk about one thing, animal or person. We do not add 's' when the verb is negative.
- Exercise 6: Work with the whole class first, making sentences about what students do or do not do on Saturdays before they write their own examples.

Spelling

For verbs ending in 'sh', 'tch', 'x' add '**es**' in the present tense.
*she wash**es*** *she catch**es*** *she mix**es***
For *go* and *do* also add '**es**': *she go**es*** *she do**es***

Choose verbs from the box to complete the story.

watch brush switch
do wash go relax

Every day Grandma __does__ a lot of housework.
She ________ the clothes, and she ________ the floor. Then she ________ shopping. In the evening she ________ with Grandpa.
She ________ on the television and ________ her favourite programme.

Word work: alphabetical order

a b c d e f g h i j k l m n o p q r s t u v w x y z

In a dictionary words are listed in **alphabetical order**.
The word *book* comes before the word *computer*.

WB 3 p137

1 Which words come first in a dictionary?

1 story, poem
2 librarian, computer
3 student, teacher
4 turtle, spider
5 football, basketball
6 week, day

2 Put these words into alphabetical order.

Example: *frog, lizard, monkey, snake*

1	monkey	frog	lizard	snake
2	banana	mango	apple	pineapple
3	car	taxi	plane	bicycle
4	door	window	chair	table
5	football	marbles	cricket	swimming

- **Word work:** Show students examples of words in alphabetical order, in a dictionary or in an index like the one at the back of this book. Discuss why we write words in alphabetical order (*to make them easier to find*).
- Remind students that we look at the first letter of each word to work out which comes first.

If words begin with the same letter, we look at the *second* letter to put them in alphabetical order.
The word ***pl**ay* comes before ***po**em.*

3 **Which of these words come first in a dictionary?**

1 poem, prayer
2 school, student
3 teacher, table
4 blackboard, backpack
5 information, important
6 fiction, fact

Writing: personal information

1 **Study the information in the application form.**

WB 3 p118

LIBRARY APPLICATION FORM	
1 Name	Brianna George
2 Date of birth	21st September, 2011
3 Name of parent	Carla George
4 Address	PO Box 137, Mountain View
5 Name of school	St. Mary's Primary School
Signed Carla George (mother)	**Date:** 12/10/2016

2 **Copy these headings. Write information about yourself under each heading.**

1 Name
2 Date of birth
3 Name of parent
4 Address
5 Name of school

Remember!
Always give correct information when you complete a form.

WB 3 p118

- **Writing:** Students can practise giving personal information correctly. They do not need to copy the application form. The Workbook contains application forms for them to complete.

Unit 4 Tortoise Tries to Fly

Get ready

Which stories do you know about animals?
Which one do you like best? Why?

Reading

Tortoise Tries to Fly

Once, Tortoise lived by a river near a cliff. He had a shell which was as smooth as a pebble. The birds often flew down and looked at themselves in Tortoise's shell.

"My shell is like a mirror," Tortoise boasted. He watched the birds flying high in the sky. He was envious of them.

"I wish I could fly like you," he sighed.

One day, Eagle swooped down. "I am having a party for all the birds," he said. "Would you like to come?"

"Yes, I would, but I can't fly," said Tortoise sadly.

Crow heard him. "I have an idea," he said. "We will give you some of our feathers. If you stick them to your shell, you will be able to fly."

Soon, Tortoise had a huge pile of feathers. When he stuck them on, he looked very strange indeed.

- **Get ready:** After students discuss their favourite animal stories, ask them what they learn from these stories to introduce the concept of stories with a 'moral'.
- Pre-reading: Students might recognise the story from the pictures. If so, get them to retell the story orally before reading. After reading they can compare their predictions with what they have read.

“How do I look?” he asked the birds.

“Like one of us,” said Crow.

“Let’s go to the top of the cliff,” said Flamingo.

“Jump!” said Macaw.

Tortoise was scared. He shut his eyes and jumped.

“Heeelp!” he cried as he fell towards the ground. CRASH! His beautiful shell broke into little pieces.

A flock of birds flew down to help him. They picked up the pieces and glued them together. Tortoise thanked them for helping him.

Tortoise’s shell was not smooth any more. It was rough and cracked. If you look at a tortoise today, you can still see the cracks.

1 Why was Tortoise proud of his shell?

2 Who invited Tortoise to a party?

3 What happened when Tortoise jumped off the cliff?

4 How many different birds spoke to Tortoise? What kind of birds were they?

5 How did the birds help Tortoise?

6 Which of these words can be used to describe Tortoise?

boastful brave vain clever helpful

7 How do you think Tortoise felt at the end of the story?

a) He was proud of his new shell.
b) He was grateful to the birds.
c) He was angry with the birds.

8 Do you try to help your friends? In what way?

- **Comprehension,** QAR: Discuss with students where they will find answers to the questions.
- Question 6 introduces the idea of **character**. Help students to find **evidence** in the story which reveals Tortoise’s character, e.g. ask ‘What makes you think Tortoise is boastful?’
- Question 8 can lead into a discussion of the **lesson** to be learnt from this story, e.g. *Don’t try to be like other people. / Help your friends.*

Story grammar

Most stories are made up of the following:

Setting: Where the story takes place.
Characters: Who takes part in the story.
Plot: What happens in the story.

Speaking and listening: story plan

Discuss how to complete the story plan.

Title of story	Tortoise tries to fly
Setting	
Characters	
Plot	Beginning: Middle: End:

Language: sentences

A **sentence** is a group of words which makes sense.
Tortoise was envious of the birds. ✓
A party for all the birds. ✗

1 Which of these are sentences?

1 Some of our feathers.
2 I can't fly.
3 As smooth as a pebble.
4 Flying high in the sky.
5 Eagle swooped down.
6 Tortoise was scared.

- **Speaking and listening:** Give students time to discuss the story plan, then complete the plan on the board with the whole class.
- **Language:** Exercise 1: Ask your students to say why some words are sentences and others are not.

2 Write these sentences correctly.

WB 3 p69

Remember!
A sentence begins with a **capital letter** and ends with a **full stop**.

1 the birds helped Tortoise → The birds helped Tortoise.
2 tortoise wanted to fly
3 he stuck feathers on his shell
4 we should always help our friends
5 my favourite story character is Anansi
6 you can find many books in a library

This is a **statement** (a telling sentence).
Tortoise lived by the river.
This is a **question** (an asking sentence).
Would you like to come to my party?

3 Which of these are statements? Which are questions?

WB 3 p68

1 Do you often read stories?
2 We sometimes read stories in class.
3 I like reading stories about animals.
4 Can tortoises fly?
5 The birds are having a party.
6 Would you like to go to the party?

Who are the characters in the story?
What happened first?
Which birds helped Tortoise?
How did Tortoise try to fly?
Why did his shell break?

We can use different words to ask questions.

4 Complete the questions.

1 What did Tortoise stick on his shell?
2 ________ invited Tortoise to a party?
3 ________ bird had red feathers?
4 ________ do tortoises have cracks in their shells?
5 ________ did Tortoise feel as he fell off the cliff?
6 ________ did he say as he fell down?

- Exercise 2: Remind students how sentences are punctuated. Get them to identify sentences in the reading text.

DA Some students can write answers to fewer questions to Exercises 1 and 3 according to ability.

5 **Make up two questions about the picture. Give your questions to a partner to answer.**

Write your questions and your partner's answers.
Remember to use full stops and question marks.

> We use an **exclamation mark** when someone has strong feelings or is shouting.
> *Help!* *Well done!* *That's amazing!*

WB 3 p69

6 **Write the sentences with correct punctuation.**
There are two statements, two questions and two exclamations.

1 Hurry up
2 Is this book yours
3 What a surprise
4 Where is your friend
5 You are very kind
6 Tortoise was scared

Word work: more about nouns

> We can put nouns into **groups**.
> **birds:** crow, macaw, flamingo
> **animals:** tortoise, monkey, horse

1 **Which nouns are the odd ones out?**

1	cow	goat	whale	horse
2	teacher	church	doctor	policeman
3	chair	table	kitchen	cupboard
4	potato	melon	banana	pawpaw
5	nose	mouth	foot	ear

- Exercises 5 and 6: Get students to identify questions, statements and exclamations in the story on pages 26–27.
- **Word work:** Students practise classifying nouns. In Exercise 1, ask them to explain their choices, e.g. *Whale is the odd one out as it is the only animal which lives in the sea.*

A **collective noun** refers to a group of people, animals or things.
*A **flock** of birds.*

2 Which word in each list is the name of the group?

A	B	C
shorts	bread	football
dress	food	swimming
clothes	meat	cricket
socks	milk	sports

3 Find the collective nouns.

1 The whole class loved the story.
2 There was a swarm of bees in the tree.
3 The crowd waited for the match to start.
4 I picked a bunch of flowers for my mother.
5 The team trains every day.

Collective nouns for you to learn
a **flock** of birds
a **herd** of goats
a **swarm** of bees
a **class** of children
a **bunch** of flowers
a **team** of footballers
a **library** of books
a **crowd** of people

WB 3 p30

Writing: plan a story

Planning

1 Plan a story about a helpful animal.

- Choose an animal to be the main character in your story.
- Choose the other animals in the story.
- Copy the story table. Use it to help you plan your story.

WB 3 p124

Title of story	
Setting	
Characters	
Plot	Beginning: Middle: End

2 Tell each other your stories.

- Say what you liked about your partner's story.
- Suggest how it could be improved.

- Collective nouns: Explain that we do not always need to name the people or things in the group, e.g. *There was a **crowd** outside the sports ground*. Singular verbs are generally used with collective nouns.
- Writing: **planning** is an important **pre-writing** skill. Focus on planning in this unit.

DA Some students may be able to write their stories according to ability.

Unit 5 Clean-up Day

Get ready

Who helps to keep your classroom tidy?

Why is it important to keep the classroom tidy?

Reading

Clean-up Day

Alyssa's teacher, Mr. John, looked very stern when he came into the classroom.

"I am disappointed in you," he told the class. "The classroom was a mess yesterday. There was a lot of paper on the floor. Many of you did not put your books away. What do you think we should do about it?"

Joel put up his hand. "We should take turns to clean the classroom at the end of the day."

"No, I disagree. That is unfair," said Alyssa's friend, Neesha. "I don't want to pick up someone else's litter."

"I have a better idea," said Tyler. "In my brother's school they have tidiness monitors. They check the classroom every day. If anyone drops litter, they ask them to pick it up."

"Do you think that is a good idea?" Mr. John asked the class. Most of the students nodded their heads.

The next day, the students voted for tidiness monitors. They chose Tyler and Alyssa.

- **Reading:** Before reading, help students to **draw inferences** from the picture. Ask: *What does it tell you about the teacher? What do you think he is saying to his students?*

At the end of the week, Alyssa and Tyler reported to Mr. John. "Everyone helped to keep the classroom tidy this week, but yesterday we discovered a lot of litter in the schoolyard. Some students ate their lunch there and they left bottles, paper and plastic bags on the ground."

"Thank you for telling me," said Mr. John. "I think we need a school clean-up day. Will you help me plan it?"

1 What kind of litter did Mr. John find in the classroom? Mr. John found paper on the floor.

2 What kind of litter did Alyssa and Tyler find in the schoolyard? Alyssa and Tyler found bottles paper and plastic bags in the schoolyard.

3 Why did the students vote? The students voted so they could deside who would be their tidiness monitor.

4 Mr. John looked very *stern*. This means that he was:

a) vexed. **b)** pleased. **c)** unwell.

5 Why do you think the girls said, "That is unfair"? They said that is unfair because they did not want to pick up other peoples litter.

6 Do you think that Mr. John was pleased with Alyssa and Tyler? Why? I think he was pleased with them because they did a good job as tidiness monitors.

7 What would you do if you saw another student dropping litter? I would tell a Teach teacher that someone was dropping litter.

8 What do you think a tidiness monitor should do? Make a list. I think a tidiness monitor should make sure the school is tidy, tell a teacher if some is littering and pick up garbage when the school or class is dirty.

- Comprehension: To answer questions 4–6, students must **draw inferences**. They cannot find the answers directly in the text, but can work them out from their understanding of what they have read.
- After reading: Discuss with students the **problem** of litter. Ask: *What could you do to **solve** the problem? Do you think that having tidiness monitors is a good idea?*

HW

Speaking and listening: making plans

1 **Plan a school clean-up day.**

Talk about what you plan to do. Use these headings to help you.

2 **Tell another pair of students about your plans.**

Language: pronouns

Pronouns are words we use instead of nouns.

Nouns ➔ ***Alyssa and Tyler*** *picked up* ***the bottles****.*

Pronouns ➔ ***They*** *picked* ***them*** *up.*

1 **Find five different pronouns in the story on pages 32–33.**

he, you, his, we and they

2 **Which words are pronouns in this story?**

Example: they

The students were busy on clean-up day. They collected all the litter. They put it in plastic sacks. When the sacks were full, they carried them to the garbage bins. Then Alyssa went to get a broom. She asked the other girls to help her sweep the yard. When the yard was clean, she called Mr. John. He told the students that he was very pleased with them.

- **Speaking and listening:** After students have discussed their plans, copy the web onto the board. Complete it as a class exercise.

DA Some students may be able to complete the web independently.

- **Language:** Exercise 1: Write two or three sentences from the story on the board and help students identify the pronouns. Then let them continue the exercise on their own.

Some pronouns usually come *before* the verb.
***I** am disappointed.* ***We** disagree.*

WB 3 p39

3 **Replace the underlined nouns with a pronoun from the box.**

Example: Mr. John looked stern. ➔ *He looked stern.*

1 Alyssa and Tyler were tidiness monitors.
They were tidiness monitors.
2 Tyler's brother goes to a different school.
He goes to a different school.
3 Some students are very untidy.
They are very untidy.
4 Josh and I helped to tidy the classroom.
We helped to tidy the classroom.
5 The litter was under the tree.
I was under the tree.
6 The bottles were broken.
They were broken.
7 My sister never clears up.
She never cleans up.
8 My English book was under my desk.
It was under my desk

These words usually come *before* verbs

I	it
you	we
he	they
she	

Some pronouns usually come **after** the verb.
*I saw **them** yesterday.* *He told **me** the news.*

4 **Replace the underlined nouns with pronouns.**

Example: My brother could not find his pen. ➔
My brother could not find it.

1 My brother put his books on the table.
My brother put it on the table.
2 He looked for his school bag.
He looked for it.
3 Kayla helped Grandma in the kitchen.
Kayla helped her in the kitchen.
4 Grandpa told Joel and me a story.
Grandpa told us a story
5 I saw my friends in the shop.
I saw them in the shop.
6 We gave Daddy a present.
We gave him a present.
7 I invited Tara and Emma to my party.
I invited them to my party
8 Mommy phoned Auntie Marie last night.
Mommy phoned her last night.

These words usually come *after* verbs

me	it
you	us
him	them
her	

- Pronouns in the first group are **subject** pronouns. In the second group, they are **object** pronouns. Students may find these terms confusing. At this stage, it is easier to define them as pronouns which come 'before' and 'after' the verb.
- Exercises 3–4: Point out that a pronoun can replace a group of words, e.g. *my English book = it.*

5 Choose the correct pronouns to replace the underlined nouns.

Example: Dwayne helped his brother. → He *helped his brother.*

1 Marie collected the books. (She / Her)
2 She put the books on the shelves. (they / them)
3 Sam and I will clear up. (We / Us)
4 Esther loves her new tablet. (it / them)
5 Grandma gave my brother and me a present. (we / us)
6 I thanked Grandma for the present. (she / her)

6 Use pronouns from the box to replace the underlined nouns.

he him she her it them

It was Grandma's birthday. Pearl gave Grandma some flowers. Grandma put the flowers in a vase. Pearl put the vase on the table, but the vase fell over and broke. Grandpa came in and saw the mess. Grandpa helped Pearl clear the mess up. Pearl thanked Grandpa for helping her. Pearl told Grandma she was sorry.

Word work: synonyms

Synonyms are words which are similar in meaning.
*Mr. John looked very **stern**.*
*Mr. John looked very **cross**.*
Stern and **cross** are synonyms.

WB 3 p82

1 Which words mean the same as the words in bold?

1 The students **selected** Tyler to be a tidiness monitor.
a) wanted b) chose c) liked

2 Mr. John **congratulated** the students for keeping the classroom tidy.
a) punished b) checked c) praised

3 Alyssa and her friends **collected** all the garbage in the yard.
a) dropped b) picked up c) destroyed

4 Mr. John was **delighted** with the students' results.
a) pleased b) disappointed c) vexed

- Exercise 6: Help students understand that they do not need to repeat the names in the story if it is clear who is being talked about. Read both versions out for them to compare.
- **Word work:** Explain that synonyms are similar in meaning, but do not have to be exactly the same.

2 **Choose synonyms from this list to replace the underlined words.**

Example: *The students tidied the classroom* daily.

began tired loudly came in daily delicious hurt huge

1 The students tidied the classroom each day.
2 There was an enormous pile of garbage in the yard.
3 In the evening it started to rain.
4 After the clean-up day the students were exhausted.
5 Everyone was quiet when the Principal entered.
6 My mother prepared some tasty snacks for us.
7 The students were all talking noisily.
8 I injured my knee when I fell over.

Writing: drafting

Imagine that you had a clean-up day at your school. Write a report.

1 **Plan your report. Use these questions to help you.**

- **When:** When was the clean-up day?
  The clean-up day was on Friday January 14, 2021.
- **Who:** Who helped clean up?
  Everyone in the class helped to clean-up
- **Where:** Where did you clean up?
  We cleaned the whole school.
- **What:** What did you do?
  I cleaned in the classroom.

2 **Write the *first draft* of your report.**

3 **Read your reports to one another. Ask each other these questions.**

- Are my sentences clear?
- How can I make it better?

Listen to each other's suggestions.

4 **Make changes to your report to improve it.**

- Planning: Explain to your students that they must use their imagination to write about clean-up day. They can use the ideas they discussed in the 'Speaking and listening' exercise on page 34. Of course, if you have had a clean-up day at your school, they can write about that.
- Drafting: This is the second stage of the writing process. Students use what they prepared in the pre-writing stage to write a first draft. The next stage will be for students to revise their first draft.

Unit 6 Steel Band Jump Up

Get ready

What kind of music do you like to listen to?
Why do you like this kind of music?

Reading

Steel Band Jump Up

I put my ear to the ground,
And I hear the steel-band sound.
Ping pong! Ping pong!
Music deep, rhythm sweet.
I'm dancing, tracking the beat:
Like a seashell's ringing song.
Ping pong! Ping pong!
Moving along, moving along,
High and low, up and down,
Ping pong! Ping pong!
Pan beating singing, round and round,
Ping pong! Ping pong!

by Faustin Charles

- **Get ready:** Ask students what they notice about the way the words are set out on the page. *(Short lines which suggest this is a poem.)*
- **Reading:** Talk about the features of a poem, e.g. *rhymes, repetition, rhythm*. Clap this out as you read the poem aloud.

1 How do you know that this is a poem?
2 What does the poet describe?
3 What makes the sound 'Ping pong!'?
4 Find three pairs of rhyming words.
5 What does the poet compare the steel-band sound to?
   a) The sound of people singing.
   b) The sound you can hear in a seashell.
   c) The beat of dance music.
6 Which different actions can you find in the poem?
7 How do you think the poet feels when he hears a steel band playing?
8 What do you like best about this poem?

Remember!
Poems often have:
- short lines
- rhymes
- repetition

Speaking and listening: recite a poem

1 Work in groups. Prepare a group recitation of the poem.

- Practise reading the poem aloud.
- Discuss how to act out the poem. Include sounds and actions, e.g. *clapping, dancing*.
- Decide who will recite the poem and who will make the sounds and actions.
- Practise your recitation.

2 Present your recitation to the class.

- **Speaking and listening:** Get students to review the group recitations (**peer evaluation**). Ask questions to help them with their review, e.g. *Did the group recite clearly? Did they make it sound interesting? Did you like the sounds and actions?*

Features of poems: rhyming words

WB 3 p115

1 Find and write the rhyming pairs in these lists.

- moon room spoon shoot roof cool
- boat hoot flat close foam nose
- call smell pole small bell hole
- train sail soil tail rain tall

Remember!
In the poem on page 38 **ground** and **sound** are rhyming words.

2 Complete the sentences with words which rhyme with the underlined words.

Example: *I like to play all* day.

1 I can see three birds in a ________.
2 There are five bees in the ________.
3 The farmer hit his toe with a ________.
4 The frog is sitting on a ________.
5 The cook is looking in a ________.
6 I am going to bake a ________.

Language: present continuous

To say what is happening **now**, we add '**ing**' to verbs.
dance → dancing *play → playing*
We use **am**, **is** or **are** before the verb:
I ***am*** *dancing. The band* ***is*** *playing.*

1 Find three more verbs ending in 'ing' in the poem. HW
Dancing, thacking and moving

WB 3 p59

2 Complete the sentences with *am*, *is* or *are*. HW

Example: *We* are *listening to the music.*

1 We are listening to the music.
2 I am reading a story.
3 Grandpa is telling a story.
4 Mommy is going shopping.
5 My brother and I are watching television.
6 Anna is washing her hands.

- Rhyming words: Get students to read the words in Exercise 1 aloud to help them identify the rhymes.
- Present continuous: Usage in standard English differs from dialect. Give your students plenty of practice in using *am/is/are* with verbs to say what is happening now.

3 **Write sentences about the pictures. Use the verbs in the box.**

WB 3 p60

jumping paint read play eat sing

Example: The girl is jumping.

1

2

3

4

5

6

Verbs ending in 'e' drop the 'e' before adding '**ing**':

*make → mak**ing**, move → mov**ing***

Many verbs double the last letter before adding '**ing**':

*stop → sto**pping**, run → ru**nning***

4 **Add 'ing' to these verbs. Make three lists.**

race look drop bake swim watch smell put taste plan bite tell stroke do have win

look → looking watch →	race → racing	drop → dropping

- **Language:** You may wish to explain that we double the final consonant for verbs which are spelt consonant + vowel + consonant.
- Practise the present continuous by asking students questions about what they can see around them, e.g. *What is Dwayne doing? Who is sitting next to Keisha?*

5 **Complete the poem.**

The wind is blowing ________. (blow)
The trees ________________. (sway)
The waves ________________. (crash)
The clouds ________________. (race)
The birds ________________. (fly)
The children ________________. (run)
The storm ________________. (come)

Word work

Sounds

The sound of some words match what the words mean.
Ping pong! Ping pong!
These words sound like the noise of a steel band.

WB 3 p90 **Match the sound words with the descriptions.**

~~buzz~~ ~~hiss~~ ~~pop~~ ~~whack~~ ~~growl~~ ~~crunch~~

1 a balloon bursting → pop
2 a fierce dog → growl
3 bees in a hive → buzz
4 a snake catching a mouse → hiss
5 a cricketer hitting a ball → whack
6 a dog eating a bone → crunch

A

- **Word work:** You may wish to tell students that these 'sound' words have a very long name (onomatopoeia).
- Get them to give their own examples, e.g. *Pop! Bang!* Remember that animal noises are often examples of onomatopoeia too, e.g. *Quack!*

Plurals

Fill the gaps with the plural forms of the nouns.

Example: *Kayla put her* books *on the* shelves. (book / shelf)

1 The _______ opened the _______. (child / box)
2 The naughty _______ stole the _______. (monkey / toy)
3 The _______ bought ten _______ of bread. (woman / loaf)
4 The _______ broke most of the _______. (girl / glass)
5 Mom bought _______ and _______ at the market. (cherry / plum)
6 There were some _______ in the _______. (mouse / cupboard)

Word work: context

Which words mean the same as the underlined words?

1 Mr. John was annoyed when the students dropped litter in the yard.
a) pleased **b)** excited **c)** vexed

2 Grandma looked everywhere for the missing keys.
a) heavy **b)** lost **c)** valuable

3 The wealthy man bought an expensive new car.
a) poor **b)** rich **c)** old

Writing

Write a report about an event you attended.

1 **Plan your report. Use these questions to help you.**
- Which event did you attend?
- When and where did it take place?
- Who went with you?
- What did you do?
- Did you enjoy the event? Why?

2 **Write the first draft of your report.**

3 **Read what you have written.**
- How could you make it better?
- Check the punctuation and spelling.

Revise your report to make it better.

- **Writing:** Students can discuss the questions in pairs or write notes independently.

DA Some students may need extra support. Work with them in a group to help them generate ideas for their reports.

Unit 7 Anansi Stories

Get ready

Who is your favourite story character?
What are some of the things he or she does?
Why do you like this character?

Reading

Anansi Stories

Once, Tiger was king of the forest. Even the stories the animals told were called the Tiger Stories. Anansi wanted the stories for himself. He went to see Tiger.

"Many things are named after you, Mr. Tiger. Nothing is named after me," he said. "Please let the animals call the stories the Anansi Stories."

Tiger decided to play a trick on Anansi. "Bring me Mr. Snake alive, and I will give you the stories." The other animals laughed. How could a little spider bring back Snake alive?

Anansi thought carefully. The next day he went to see Snake.

"Good morning, Mr. Snake," he said. "Everyone says that you are as long as the branch of a tree. I don't believe them."

"Why not?" said Snake. "I am longer than that bamboo."

Anansi cut a long branch of bamboo. "Stretch out beside this branch," he said.

Snake lay down beside the branch.

Pre-reading: Before starting to read, get your students to predict the story from the pictures. If they know the story, let them tell you what they remember about it. Encourage them to **draw inferences** about the characters from the pictures, e.g. *What does the picture tell us about Tiger?*

"Mr. Snake," said Anansi. "How will I know that you are longer than the branch? When I look at your head, you will crawl up the branch. When I look at your tail, you will crawl down."

"Tie my tail to the branch then," said Snake.

Anansi tied Snake's tail onto the branch. "Close your eyes and stretch out your head."

Snake closed his eyes and stretched out as far as he could. Quickly Anansi tied Snake's head to the branch. Now Anansi could carry Snake to Tiger.

Tiger could not believe his eyes when Anansi brought Snake to him, but he kept his promise. From that day on, the stories were called Anansi Stories.

1 What did the animals call the stories they told?

2 What did Tiger ask Anansi to bring him?

3 Why did the other animals laugh at Anansi?

4 How did Anansi trick Snake?

5 When Tiger saw Snake tied to a branch, he <u>could not believe his eyes</u>. This means that:

a) Tiger could not see very well.

b) Tiger was afraid of Snake.

c) Tiger was very surprised.

6 Choose words from this list to describe Anansi.

clever	dangerous	cunning	silly	proud

7 Do you think Tiger was pleased when Anansi brought him Snake? Why? Why not?

8 Which character do you like best in this story? Why?

- Comprehension: Ask students to discuss the answers to some of the questions in pairs, e.g. questions 4, 6, 7 and 8. Remind them that when they express an opinion, they must justify it with evidence from the text.

DA Get students to work with different partners from time to time, according to ability.

Speaking and listening: describing characters

Describe the character Anansi.

He has eight legs.

He plays tricks.

- What does he look like?
- How does he behave?
- What are some of the things he does?

Choose another character from a story. Describe this character.

Language

Past tense

We add '**d**' or '**ed**' to most verbs to show that something happened in the past.

*Tiger decide**d** to play a trick on Anansi.*

*The animals laugh**ed** at Anansi.*

WB 3 p52

1 **Write the past tense of these verbs.**

Example: ask → asked

asked listened crawled

ask	listen	crawl
stretch	live	close

stretch lived closed

2 **Use the verbs you made to complete the story.**

Anansi went to see Snake. Snake __lived__ in a hole. He __listened__ carefully to Anansi. Then he __crawled__ slowly out of his hole. Anansi __asked__ him to lie down beside the branch. Snake __closed__ his eyes. He lay down and __streched__ out as far as he could.

- **Speaking and listening:** Before students work in pairs, brainstorm adjectives describing Anansi.

Some verbs double the last letter before adding '**ed**'.
stop ➔ stopped: *The animals soon **stopped** laughing.*

3 Change these sentences to the past tense.

WB 3 p52

Example: *Matthew* spotted *a snake in the bushes.*

1. Matthew spots a snake in the bushes.
2. All the animals clap for Anansi.
3. Lisa trips on a stone.
4. Kayla drops her books on the floor.
5. The frog hops from one leaf to another.
6. The lambs skip along beside their mothers.

If the verb ends in a consonant followed by 'y', change the 'y' to 'i' and add '**ed**'.
carry ➔ carried: *Anansi **carried** Snake to Tiger.*
If the verb ends in a vowel followed by 'y', just add '**ed**'.
stay ➔ stayed: *Snake **stayed** in his hole all day.*

4 Write the past tenses of these verbs.

reply pray worry study delay annoy

5 Complete the sentences with past tense verbs.

Example: *Anansi* envied *Tiger.* *(envy)*

1. Tiger ________ to play a trick on Anansi. (try)
2. The dog ________ the bone in the garden. (bury)
3. The children ________ outside all day. (play)
4. We all ________ the story Grandpa told us. (enjoy)
5. My sister ________ when she broke her new toy. (cry)
6. The tall tree ________ in the wind. (sway)

- Doubling letters: You may wish to explain that for verbs consisting of consonant + vowel + consonant we double the last letter before adding 'ed'.

Irregular past tense verbs

Some verbs are **irregular** in the past tense.
tell ➔ told: *The animals* ***told*** *each other stories.*
go ➔ went: *Anansi* ***went*** *to see Snake.*

WB 3 p53

1 Find the past tense of the verbs in the box on the right in the story on pages 48–49.

cut	think	say
lie down	bring	keep

2 Learn the past tenses of the verbs in the box.

- Choose four verbs.
- Write a sentence with each one.

3 Retell the story in the past tense.

Example: Mr. and Mrs. Goat went…

Mr. and Mrs. Goat go to market. Mrs. Goat takes a basket with her. At the market they meet some of their friends. Mrs. Goat buys some tomatoes. She pays the trader. When she goes home, she makes some delicious tomato soup. Mr. Goat eats it all.

Irregular past tense	
begin	began
buy	bought
come	came
eat	ate
give	gave
go	went
have	had
make	made
meet	met
pay	paid
see	saw
tell	told
take	took

4 Complete the sentences with past tense verbs.

Not all the verbs are irregular.

1 Mr. Goat ________ Mrs. Goat some money. (give)
2 Mrs. Goat ________ a lot of tomatoes in her basket. (have)
3 She ________ to cook lunch. (hurry)
4 Mr. Goat ________ the tomato soup. (enjoy)
5 Grandpa ________ me an exciting story. (tell)
6 Jack ________ me to his party. (invite)
7 Most of my friends ________ to his party. (come)
8 I ________ Jack's present. (wrap)

- There are hundreds of irregular past tense verbs. Your students can record and learn them as they come across them. Get them to make example sentences with these verbs, as it is easier to learn them in context.

Word work: root words

Some words are made up of more than one part.
stays = stay + 's'   *stayed* = stay + 'ed'   *staying* = stay + 'ing'

Stay is a **root word**. 's', 'ed' and 'ing' are **suffixes**.
We add suffixes to change the meaning of words.

What is the root word?

WB 3 p74

Example: *laughs* *laughing* *laughed* ➔ root word: laugh

1	stretching	stretches	stretched
2	worries	worrying	worried
3	promised	promising	promises
4	trots	trotted	trotting

Writing: revising

Choose a character in a story you both know well.

1 **Copy the web and make notes about this character.**
Do not copy the words in the shaded boxes below.

WB 3 p134

- Name of your character
  - What your character looks like
  - What kind of a person he or she is
  - What your character's home is like
  - Some of the things your character does

2 **Each of you writes about the character you chose. When you have finished, show your work to your partner.**

3 **Tell each other what you like about the writing. Discuss how you could make it better.**

4 **Make changes to your writing to improve it.**

- **Writing:** After students write their first draft, **revising** is the next part of the writing process. After writing, students can **evaluate** each other's work. To guide the process, tell them to find one thing they like and suggest one thing to improve. They can then go back to their work and revise it.

Unit 8 The Class Visit

Get ready

Which places would you like to visit?
What would you like to see and do there?

Reading

The Class Visit

Address of person writing, and date

PO Box 106,
Georgetown,
St. Vincent.

20th March, 2016

Greeting → Dear Kellie,

Body of letter →

How are you? Did you get the card I sent you for Christmas? We all miss you very much at school.

Last week, Mrs. Turner took our class to the Botanical Gardens in Kingstown. Did you know that the gardens are 250 years old?

A guide met us at the entrance. He showed us around the gardens. The gardens are very large. There are hundreds of trees and plants there. We did not have time to see them all.

- **Get ready:** Introduce the theme of this unit by discussing visits students may have made, e.g. school visit or visits with family or church.
- **Reading:** Help students to identify the **five parts of a letter: address and date, greeting, body of letter, closing and signature**. Conventions for writing addresses vary. You may wish to use different punctuation from that shown above.

After that, we went to see the St. Vincent parrots. They were very colourful and made a lot of noise. Then we sat in the shade under the trees, and ate our lunch. I had cheese sandwiches, fruit and juice.

Before we went home, the guide showed us the famous breadfruit tree. This tree is descended from the very first breadfruit tree planted in the Caribbean.

We all thought it was a really interesting visit. Mrs. Turner promised to take us there again one day.

Have you visited any interesting places in the USA? I would love to hear about them. Come back and visit us soon!

Your friend, ← closing

Lisette ← signature

1 Where are the Botanical Gardens?

2 How old are the gardens?

3 Who met the students at the entrance to the gardens?

4 Why were the students not able to see all the trees and plants?

5 Why do you think the students ate their lunch under the trees?

6 Who is Kellie?

a) A teacher at Lisette's school.
b) A girl who used to go to Lisette's school.
c) One of the students in Lisette's class.

7 Which part of the visit do you think was the most interesting? Give reasons to explain your choice.

8 Where would you like to go on a class visit? Why?

- Discuss **question words** with your students. Point out that they will probably find the answers to 'what', 'where', 'when' or 'who' questions directly in the text. 'Why' questions are usually **inferential questions**. They need to think and search to find the answers.

Speaking and listening: describing a visit

1 Answer these questions about Lisette's letter.

- Where did Mrs. Turner take her class?
- What did they do first?
- What did they do next?

2 Make more questions about the class visit. Use different question words.

3 Each of you thinks of an interesting visit you made. Take turns to ask each other questions about the visit.

Language

Past tense

Was and **were**

For one person, thing or animal, we use **was**.

*The visit **was** really interesting.*

For more than one person, thing or animal, we use **were**.

*The parrots **were** very colourful.*

Note: With **you** we use **were:** *You **were** very lucky.*

1 Write six sentences.

Example: The students were thirsty.

WB 3 p54

The students		old.
The breadfruit tree		happy.
The parrots	was	thirsty.
Lisette and her friends	were	tired.
I		pleased.
Mrs. Turner		noisy.

- **Speaking and listening:** Give students plenty of practice in asking questions to find out information. Choose students to report to the class what they found out about their partner's visit.

2 Complete the story with *was* or *were*.

Rick ___was___ at the sports ground. It _________ midday and his friends _________ late. Then he saw them. They _________ hot and tired.

"Where _________ you?" he asked. "I _________ worried."

"We _________ on the bus. It _________ very slow."

We use 'did' with the **root form** of the verb in past tense questions:

*Where **did** the students **go** for their class visit?*

***Did** they **enjoy** the visit?*

3 Write questions.

WB 3 p55

Example: Where did the students eat their lunch?

1 where _____ the students eat their lunch
2 what _____ you do in the gardens
3 _____ they see parrots there
4 _____ you go to the beach last Saturday
5 _____ Lisette write a letter to her friend
6 when _____ Kelly go to the USA

We use ***did*** with the **root form** of the verb for **negative** sentences in the past.

*We **did not have** time to see all the trees and plants.*

4 Write negative sentences.

WB 3 p56

Example: The children did not see the parrots in the garden.

1 The children saw the parrots in the garden.
2 Kelly wrote a letter to Lisette.
3 She returned to her old school.
4 Mrs. Turner took the children to the gardens again.
5 We played under the trees.
6 I went out on the boat with my brother.

- Remind students that the **root form** of the verb is the main part of the verb. We can add endings to the base form to change its meaning, e.g. *ask – asked*.
- Get students to make up questions to ask a friend who went to visit cousins on another island.

6 Write sentences about what you did last Sunday.

- Write three sentences saying what you did.
- Write three sentences saying what you did not do.

Commas

We use **commas** when we write the date:

Monday, 15th January
20th March, 2016

1 Write these dates.

1. Your date of birth. Friday, 14th August 2012
2. The date of birth of the student sitting next to you. Wednesday, 2nd April 201
3. Today's date. Monday, 9th November 2020
4. Tomorrow's date. Tuesday, 10 November 2020
5. The date your country became independent. Wednesday, 6 August 1962

We also use **commas** at the end of each line when we write **addresses**.

46, Park Road,
Victoria,
Grenada.

2 Write these addresses correctly.

1. 22 fields lane roseau dominica (22 Fields Lane Roseau Dominica)
2. 3 market street saint john's antigua (3 Market Street Saint John's Antigua)
3. 41 beach road holetown barbados (41 Beach Road Holetown Barbados)
4. 15 central road toronto canada (15 Central Road Toronto Canada)

Remember
We use **capital letters** for the names of places and countries.

- Look back at the letter on pages 54–55 and get students to find where commas are used. Remind students that commas must also be used after the greeting and the closing.

Word work: sequencing words

1. **Read the notes Akim made about going shopping with his mother.**

- Saturday, went shopping
- market, bought fruit
- looked for new shoes
- ate ice cream
- took bus home

2. **Write about Akim's shopping trip. Use the words *first*, *next*, *then*, *after that*.**

Begin: On Saturday, Akim went shopping with his mother. First …

Writing: proofreading

Write a letter to a friend or family member about a visit you made to a place of interest.

1. **Ask each other questions to get ideas for your letter.**
   - Where did you go? When?
   - Who did you go with?
   - What did you see and do there?
   - Did you enjoy the visit? Why?

2. **Write the first draft of your letter.**
   Remember to set your letter out like the letter on pages 54–55.

3. **Revise your letter. Change it to make it better.**

WB 3 p135

4. **Proofread your letter. Use this checklist.**

Checklist for proofreading

Have I:

- used correct punctuation? ☐
- started each sentence with a capital letter? ☐
- written in full sentences? ☐
- spelt tricky words correctly? ☐

- **Writing: proofreading** is the final stage in the writing process. When students **proofread**, they check for spelling, grammar and punctuation. Work with the class to produce a list of points to remember when punctuating a letter.

Unit 9 Drinking Water-Coconut

Get ready

Look at the writing below.
Is it a poem or a story? How do you know that?

Reading

Drinking Water-Coconut

Feeling thirsty
feeling hot
nothing to cool you down
like a water-coconut

With a flick of her cutlass
market-lady will hand you one –
a sweet little hole brimming at the top
when you put it to your head
you wouldn't want it to stop

Then you'll be wondering
if there's jelly inside
ask market-lady if she wouldn't mind
she'll flick the big nut right open for you
she'll flick you a coconut spoon
to scoop with too

Feeling thirsty
feeling hot
the best thing to spend your money on
is a water-coconut

Grace Nichols

- **Get ready:** Ask students what they notice about the way the words are set out on the page. *(Short lines arranged in groups, which suggest this is a poem.)*
- **Reading:** Talk about the features of poems, e.g. verses, rhymes. Point these out as you read the poem.

1 How many verses are there in the poem?
2 Which words in the poem rhyme?
3 What does a market-lady use to open a coconut?
4 What is inside the coconut?
5 What does the word *scoop* mean? (verse 3)

a) drink **b)** dig out **c)** throw

6 What is the main idea of the poem?

a) Market-ladies sell water-coconuts in the market.

b) You can use a spoon to eat the jelly in a coconut.

c) Drinking water-coconut cools you down when you feel hot.

7 What do you do when you feel hot and thirsty?
8 Which verse of the poem do you like best? Why?

Speaking and listening

We have **five senses**. We can:

- see
- smell
- hear
- touch
- taste

In the poem the poet describes something she likes to **taste**.

1 Tell each other five things you like to taste.

2 Make sentences about the picture. Say what the children see, hear, smell, taste and touch.

Example: The girl in pink is smelling a flower.

- **Speaking and listening:** Discuss the five senses. Link the senses with different parts of the body, e.g. we use our eyes to see.
- Before students make sentences about the picture, discuss which senses it portrays, e.g. the boy eating ice cream: *taste*.

3 **Talk to your partner about things you like to taste, hear, touch and smell.**

Language

Adjectives

> **Adjectives** are words which tell us *more* about nouns.
> *The weather was **hot**. The **thirsty** boy drank the juice.*

1 **Which word in each group is an adjective?**

Ask yourself: *Which words can I use to describe a water-coconut?*

flick	juicy	money	cutlass
sweet	spoon	stop	round
jelly	market-lady	big	you

WB 3 p34 **2** **Find and write the adjective in each sentence.**

1 The weather was cool yesterday. ➔ cool
2 The baby chicks are fluffy.
3 My grandmother lives in an old house.
4 I could hear loud music.
5 My mother has a new car.
6 The students were noisy.

> **Remember!**
> Adjectives can come *before* or *after* nouns.

- **Speaking and listening:** Encourage your students to use their imagination when they talk about things they like to see, hear, touch and smell.
- Extension: Some students can make sentences about things they don't like touching or smelling.

3 **Choose adjectives from the box below to describe the nouns.**

Example: *a* tall *tree*

busy	delicious	exciting	sandy
furry	lovely	tall	fierce
shining			

1 a tree
2 a beach
3 stars
4 a kitten
5 flowers
6 a market
7 ice cream
8 a dog
9 a story

Comparative and superlative

When we compare two things we add '**-er**' to adjectives. Sometimes we have to change the spelling:

small ➔ *small**er***
happy ➔ *happi**er***

1 **Complete the sentences with the correct adjective forms.**

WB 3 p36

Example: A mouse is smaller than a cat. (*small*)

1 A cat is ________ than a mouse. (*big*)
2 It is ________ in March than in July. (*hot*)
3 Kiara's work is ________ this term. (*good*)
4 The weather was ________ yesterday. (*cold*)
5 My sister's room is ________ than mine. (*tidy*)
6 Kim's writing is ________ than Kia's. (*bad*)

2 **Make your own sentences.**

Example: A horse is bigger than a dog.

1 a horse / big / a dog
2 the pink flowers / pretty / the yellow flowers
3 Grade 4 students / noisy / Grade 3 students
4 Mr. John / thin / Mr. Brown

Comparatives for you to learn

big	bigger
busy	busier
fat	fatter
hot	hotter
noisy	noisier
pretty	prettier
sad	sadder
thin	thinner

Special forms:

good	better
bad	worse

- Exercise 3: To practise using adjectives, play a guessing game. One student describes an everyday object without naming it. Other students must guess what it is.
- Comparative and superlative: Tell students that the adjectives we use to compare people or things are called comparative adjectives.

With longer adjectives we use **more** to compare things.
*A hummingbird is **more beautiful** than a crow.*

3 Discuss these questions.

1 Which is more difficult, making a cup of tea or baking a cake?
2 Which stories are more interesting, stories about animals or stories about people?
3 Which is more expensive, a car or a bicycle?
4 Which is more intelligent, a crow or a parrot?

When we compare more than two things we add '**-est**' to adjectives.
*tall – tall**est*** *big – bigg**est***
With longer adjectives we use **most** to compare things.
*The rose is the **most beautiful** flower.*

WB 3 p37 **4 Complete the sentences with the correct adjective forms.**

Example: Rick is the biggest boy in our class.

1 Rick is the ______ boy in our class. (*big*)
2 Which is the ______ animal? (*intelligent*)
3 That was the ______ story I ever heard. (*funny*)
4 Alex painted the ______ picture. (*good*)
5 I think that mangoes are the ______ fruit. (*delicious*)
6 Saturday is the ______ day at the market. (*busy*)

Superlatives for you to learn

big	biggest
busy	busiest
fat	fattest
funny	funniest
pretty	prettiest
sad	saddest
thin	thinnest

Special forms:

good	best
bad	worst

5 Answer the questions.

1 Who is the tallest student in your class?
2 Which month is the hottest?
3 Which flower do you think is the most beautiful?
4 Who is the most famous sportsman in your country?

- Exercise 3: Encourage students to make sentences using comparative adjectives, e.g. *I think that baking a cake is more difficult than making a cup of tea.* Then compare opinions around the class.
- Exercise 5: Point out the special forms 'best' and 'worst' before students start the exercise. Get students to answer the questions orally using full sentences.

DA Some students may be able to write answers to Exercise 5.

Word work: suffixes

A **suffix** is a letter or group of letters we put at the end of words to change their meaning.
thirst + 'y' = thirsty *help + 'ful' = helpful*

1 **Copy these words and underline the suffixes. Learn how to spell them.**

grateful noisy careless powerful rainy colourful

2 **Complete each sentence with one of the above words.**

1 The ________ girl spilt the juice on the table.
2 On ________ days I stay at home.
3 The dancers wore ________ costumes.
4 The fishing boat has a ________ motor.
5 The music in the van was very ________.
6 I am very ________ for your help.

Writing: description

1 **Compare these sentences. Which are more interesting? Why?**

1 I sat under a tree in the garden.
I saw some flowers.

2 I sat under a shady green tree in the garden.
I saw some beautiful red flowers.

2 **Imagine that you are at a market. Write sentences about what you can see, hear and smell there.** WB 3 p126

3 **Read what you have written. How can you improve it? Use this checklist.**

Checklist for description
Have I:
- used interesting adjectives? ☐
- described what you can see, hear and smell? ☐
- written full sentences? ☐

- **Writing:** To **generate ideas** for the writing task, brainstorm adjectives which describe a market. Then they write their **first draft**.
- **Revising** is the next stage in the writing process. Students read through what they have written and consider how they could improve it. Get them to use a simple checklist to help them revise their work.

Unit 10 Exciting News

Get ready

Have you ever received an invitation from a friend or family member? What did this person invite you to do?

Reading

Exciting News

As soon as Mr. Jackson came home from work last Friday, he checked his emails. Daniel heard him call out, "Daniel, your Uncle Kevin has sent me an email. Come and take a look!" Daniel sat beside his father and looked at the screen. This is what he read.

Kevin Jackson 20.45 14/10/16 Re: tickets

To: garynvj-1586@CBX_A2.com
From: kevjacks1081@BCB-90.com
Subject: Tickets

Hi Gary,
How is everyone? We are all fine here. Jessica loves her new school and Joel has his first tooth.

Great news! I have three tickets for the first day of the President's Cup next Wednesday. I know you love cricket. Would you like to come? Bring Daniel with you. It's time for him to see some good matches.

It will be a thrilling day. The first match will start at 10.00 a.m. Barbados will play Guyana. We need to get there early to get good seats.

- **Reading:** Study the layout of the email and discuss the information provided at the top. You may wish to point out that the position of the closing and signature in an email differs from a letter.
- Ask students to **skim** the email to find out why Daniel's uncle wrote it. Explain that skimming means glancing over a text quickly to find out what it is about.

Come and have dinner with us after the match. Grace and I are looking forward to seeing you, and Jessica wants to play with her big cousin Daniel.

Let us know if you can come.

Best wishes to all the family.

Kevin

When Daniel finished reading, there was a broad smile on his face. "Well," said his father, "what shall I tell Uncle Kevin?"

1 Which teams will play on the first day of the President's Cup?
2 When will the match start?
3 Why is it important not to be late for the match?
4 Who do you think Jessica and Joel are?
5 Do you think Daniel has been to an important match before? Why do you say that?
6 What is the main reason why Daniel's Uncle Kevin sent this email?
   a) To ask Daniel and his father to come to dinner.
   b) To invite Daniel and his father to a cricket match.
   c) To send news about his family.
7 Would you like to go to a sports event? Which one? Give reasons for your choice.
8 Which is your favourite sport? Why?

- Comprehension: Remind students not to pick answers straight out of the text, e.g. in Question 3 they must change the pronoun: ***They*** *must get there early to get good seats*.

Speaking and listening: planning a visit

Imagine that you saw this poster at your school about a concert.

Role play

- Student A plays the role of a student. He or she wants to go to the concert.
- Student B plays the role of the mother.

Begin:

STUDENT A: Mommy, I saw a poster about a school dance contest. Can we go?

STUDENT B: Tell me more about it. When is it?

Continue the dialogue.

Language

Future tense

WB 3 p57

1 Read the notes from Daniel's diary. Write sentences about what he will do.

Example: He will get up at 6.00 a.m.

Saturday, October 4th
6.00 a.m. Get up
6.30 a.m. Leave home
7.00 a.m. Take bus to Bridgetown
8.00 a.m. Meet Uncle Keith
8.30 a.m. Arrive at Kensington Oval
10.00 a.m. Watch cricket match
Return home late!

2 Answer these questions.

1 When will you go home today?
2 What will you do after school?
3 Where will you go on the weekend?
4 What will you be when you grow up?

- **Speaking and listening:** Student A plays the role of the child who saw the poster. Student B plays the role of the mother. Before starting the role play, ask students to suggest the questions they need to ask in order to **elicit information** about the poster.

Owning things

These words tell us who owns something. They are **adjectives**:

my your his her its our their

They go *before* nouns.

Joel has ***his*** *first tooth.*

Jessica wants to play with ***her*** *big cousin.*

1 **Complete the paragraph with** ***his, her, its*** **or** ***their*.**

WB 3 p41

Everyone was happy to see Daniel and __his__ father. Jessica showed them __her__ new toys. Joel smiled at __his__ big cousin. The dog sat under the table and wagged __its__ tail. Daniel told __his__ aunt all about the match. After dinner, Daniel and his father took __their__ things and went home. Before they left, Daniel thanked __his__ uncle for inviting them to the match.

2 **Choose the correct words to complete the sentences.**

Example: *Daddy took* __me__ *to a football match.* (me / my)

1 You can invite __your__ parents to the concert. (you / your)
2 My aunt sent __us__ an email. (us / our)
3 The girls told __their__ friends about the show. (them / their)
4 I went shopping with __my__ mother. (me / my)
5 Daniel promised not to lose __his__ ticket. (him / his)
6 Daniel's uncle asked __them__ not to be late. (them / their)

- *My, your etc*. are **possessive adjectives**. They describe nouns. Give your students a simple explanation. They do not need to know the grammatical term.
- Owning things, Exercise 1: According to ability, allow some students to find the missing words without rewriting the whole paragraph.
- Exercise 2: Work through the exercise on the board. Emphasise that we use *my, your, his, her, our, their* before nouns.

These words also tell us who owns things.
mine yours his hers ours theirs
They are **pronouns**. They do not have a noun after them.

WB 3 p42

3 Choose the correct words to complete the sentences.

Example: *These are your shoes. The shoes are* yours.

mine yours his hers ours theirs

1 These are Daniel's sneakers. They are ___his___.
2 "Is this pen ___yours___?" Mr. Adams asked Josh.
3 "Whose bag is this?" "It's ___mine___," said Mia.
4 "Please give us those books. They are ___ours___," said Grace and Kim.
5 "Are these Maria's things?" "Yes, they are ___hers___."
6 The books belong to Jason and Matt. The pencils are ___theirs___ too.

4 Complete the dialogue with the correct words.

Mom was vexed. The house was untidy. She asked Kim to help her tidy up.

MOM: Is this ___your___ (*your / yours*) backpack, Kim?
KIM: No, it isn't ___mine___ (*my / mine*). I'll ask Anna if it is ___hers___ (*her / hers*).
MOM: Are these ___your___ (*your / yours*) sneakers?
KIM: I don't think so. ___My___ (*My / Mine*) sneakers are smaller.
MOM: What about this game? Does it belong to the boys?
KIM: It must be ___theirs___ (*their / theirs*). I saw them playing with it.
MOM: Do these books belong to Anna and you?
KIM: No, we left ___our___ (*our / ours*) books on the sofa.

- *Mine, yours* etc. are **possessive pronouns.** They replace nouns. Demonstrate by collecting classroom items from different students. Ask and answer around the class, e.g. *Is this pencil yours, John? No, it's not mine. It's hers.*

Word work: syllables

Breaking words into **syllables** helps us to *read* and *spell* them.

- Two syllables: *crick/et*   *thrill/ing*
- Three syllables: *Pres/i/dent*   *in/vi/ted*

Some words have only one syllable: *tooth, match*

1 Look at Uncle Kevin's email and find:

WB 3 p75

- three words with one syllable.
- three words with two syllables.
- three words with three syllables.

2 Add three more words of your own to each list.

- Words with one syllable: girl ....
- Words with two syllables: ticket ....
- Words with three syllables: Barbados ....

Writing: write an email

1 Prepare the text of an email to send to a member of your family. Invite this person to visit you. Remember to:

- greet this person at the beginning of your email.
- invite him or her to visit you and give details, e.g. date and time.
- say what you will do.
- send your best wishes and write your name.

2 Revise the text of your email. Show it to another student. Ask him or her to check:

- you have included all the necessary information.
- you have written the information clearly.

- Emails: Discuss suitable greetings for emails to friends or relatives, e.g. *Hi! Hello!*
- Remind students that they must use correct grammar and spelling in emails.

Unit 11 Read the Label!

Get ready

Which shops do you go to when you go shopping?
What do you buy there?

Reading

- **Get ready:** Elicit the names of different shops and what can be bought there. Talk about the differences between markets and shopping malls.
- **Reading:** Ask students where they would find these texts. Discuss the **purpose** of the texts, e.g. to give you information about the products, to make you want to buy them.

Glossary

product something which is made to be sold

slogan words which make you remember a product and want to buy it

Makes your teeth tingle!

This is a slogan for toothpaste.

1 Which product might help you to do well at school?

2 Which products would you buy on a hot day?

3 Which product does not contain anything artificial?

4 *Quench your thirst* is a slogan. Find two other slogans.

5 Is the text about ice cream:

a) a recipe?

b) a label?

c) an advertisement?

6 What kind of information about the products can you find in these texts?

7 Which text do you like best? Why?

8 In which different places can you see advertisements?

- Look closely at the texts with students to find examples of **persuasive language**. Ask: *What words are used in the texts to persuade people to buy the products?*
- You may wish to point out examples of **alliteration**, e.g. *Tropical Taste*. This device is often used in slogans.

Fact and opinion

Hw f op 10/05/2021

A **fact** is a piece of information which *is* true.
Contains no artificial ingredients. Fact

An **opinion** is something we *think* is true.
Our ice creams are really tasty. Opinion

1 **Find one fact and one opinion in the labels on pages 72–73.**

Opinion - Our mangoes are the finest in the world. Fact - Made in Jamaica.

WB 3 p95 **2** **Which of these statements are facts? Which are opinions?**

1 The shop sells bread, cookies and cakes. fact
2 The cakes are really delicious. opinion
3 It is too hot to play football today. fact
4 I play football every Saturday. fact
5 "Coconut Beach Hotel" is 1 km from the airport. fact
6 "Coconut Beach" is the best hotel in the Caribbean. opinion

Speaking and listening

1 **Look at the texts on page 72 again. Discuss these questions.**

- Who would buy Mama's ice cream?
- Who would buy Krunchy Flakes?
- Who would buy Tropical Taste Mango Juice?

Adults, children or both?

2 **Which text do you think is the most attractive? Why?**

3 **Think of three other things people buy, e.g. bread. Invent slogans for them.**

- **Speaking and listening:** Students discuss the likely **audience** for the texts on pages 72–73.
- Give examples of signs and notices they may see around them, e.g. a bus timetable, road signs. Ask them who these are intended for – the audience.

Language

Articles

We use **the** before nouns for particular things or people.
The ice cream I bought at the beach

We use **a** or **an** for general things or people.
Grandma bought me ***an*** *ice cream.*

Remember!
We use **an** before nouns which begin with **vowels** (a, e, i, o, u): *an ice cream.*

1 **Complete the sentences with *a*, *an* or *the*.**

WB 3 p62

1 Mommy bought _______ box of cereal.
2 I did not like _______ new cereal.
3 Did you pay for _______ eggs?
4 I always eat _______ egg for breakfast.
5 _______ fruit was very expensive.
6 There was _______ orange in the bowl.
7 My aunt poured me _______ glass of juice.
8 Did you like _______ cake Grandma baked for you?

We use **some** when we do not give an exact quantity.
I bought ***some*** *biscuits.*

We use **any** in questions and negative sentences.
Do you have ***any*** *fruit? I don't have* ***any*** *oranges.*

2 **Complete the dialogue with *some* or *any*.**

Laura: Did you buy ___any___ mangoes?
Mom: No, they didn't have _______ mangoes at the market. I bought _______ oranges instead.
Laura: What else did you buy?
Mom: I bought _______ juice and _______ biscuits. There wasn't _______ bread left.
Laura: Did you buy _______ sweets for me?
Mom: There aren't _______ sweets in my basket. Wait a minute! Here are _______ sweets in my pocket.

- **Language:** Explain that in the sentence, '*Grandma bought me an ice cream*' we are not told which ice cream she bought so we say *an*.

Abbreviations

We use **abbreviations** to write words in a shorter way.

Road: **Rd.** *centimetre:* **cm**

We put a **full stop** after most abbreviations, but not after measurements.

We sometimes write **initials** in place of our names.

Conroy Williams **C.W.** *Pearl Chang* **P.C.**

WB 3 p86

1 Abbreviate these expressions.

Example: *300 kilograms* → 300 kg

1. 21, Coastal Road
2. South America
3. Saint Michael's Church
4. Doctor Mercy Reid
5. 100 kilometres
6. West Indies
7. Kevin John Jackson
8. 20 litres

Abbreviations for you to learn

litre	l
gram	g
centimetre	cm
kilogram	kg
kilometre	km
Street	St.
Road	Rd.
Saint	St.
North	N.
South	S.
East	E.
West	W.
Doctor	Dr.

2 Write your own name and your teacher's name. Use initials.

3 Here are some well-known abbreviations.

USA United States of America
OECS Organisation of Eastern Caribbean States
WI West Indies

Do you know any more like this?

4 Find abbreviations in the address.

Write your own address. Use as many abbreviations as you can.

- Opinions about when to use full stops after abbreviations vary. Teach students the system most commonly used in your country.
- Exercise 3: Write abbreviations commonly used in your country on the board and explain what they mean.

Word work: spelling

Tips to help you learn to spell tricky words:

- Break words into syllables:

  pro/duct *slo/gan* *break/fast*
- Underline the difficult parts of words:

  juice *listen* *instruction*

Learn to spell these words.

Break these words into syllables.

expensive advertisement natural tropical

Underline the difficult parts.

flavour guava bright litre

Writing

Remember!
Layout: how you organise the words and pictures on a page.

1 **Plan an advertisement for a product.**

- Choose a product, e.g. *a cheesy snack, sports shoes, a new computer game*.
- Think of a name for your product.
- Discuss the information you will include in your advertisement.
- Plan the layout of your advertisement.

2 **Make a rough draft of your advertisement. Show it to another pair of students. Ask them:**

WB 3 p121

- Is the information in the advertisement clear?
- What do you like about our advertisement?
- What could we improve?

3 **Revise your advertisement. Copy it onto a clean sheet of paper.**

- **Word work:** Revise the **'Look, Cover, Check'** method of learning spellings.

DA **Writing:** Put students in mixed ability pairs to create their advertisements. If possible, provide them with large sheets of paper for their advertisements. Some students may be able to invent a slogan for their product.

Unit 12 All's Well That Ends Well

Get ready

What should you remember to do when you cross a road?
Which other road safety rules do you know?

Reading

All's Well That Ends Well

Greg was only five years old. His mother did not let him go out on his own. When he went to play with his friend, Terry, his mother always went with him.

"It's too dangerous," she told him. "Many children are injured crossing the road. You could get killed."

One day Greg's mother was too busy to take him to see his friend. She told him to stay in the house and play with his toys. Greg played with his toy truck, but before long he felt bored. The front door was open so he went out into the yard.

"I know the way to Terry's house," he thought. "I'll go there on my own."

So Greg set off down the road by himself. He walked past the church and the library and came to the main road. He checked to see if any cars were coming. Then he crossed safely.

"This is easy," Greg said to himself. He went on towards Terry's house. He saw two older boys on the other side of the road playing marbles. Greg loved playing marbles.

What do you think will happen next in the story?

- **Get ready:** Take the opportunity to discuss road safety with students. Ask questions to find out what they know. What would they tell a younger brother or sister?
- **Reading:** Use the pictures to predict the story. Revise students' predictions as you read. Pause at the end of this page to ask students to predict the end of the story.

"Can I play with you?" he shouted. Without looking to left or right he dashed across the road. He did not spot a van coming round the corner.

"Look out!" the boys shouted.

A man ran out of a shop and grabbed Greg. He pulled him out of the road just in time.

"Where's your mommy?" the man asked Greg.

Greg said nothing. He was too scared. Then he saw his mother running down the road towards him.

She hugged him and said, "Thank goodness you're safe!"

1 How old is Greg?
2 Why does his mother always go with him when he goes to play with Terry?
3 Which buildings did Greg pass before he reached the main road?
4 Why did he decide to go to Terry's house on his own?
5 Why do you think Greg did not check the road before he crossed the second time?
6 Which adjective best describes Greg in this story?

careful sensible disobedient bored

7 What do you think Greg's mother will do when they get home?
8 The title of the story is 'All's Well That Ends Well'. This means:
   a) Some things went wrong and the story ended badly.
   b) Some things went wrong, but there was a happy ending.
   c) You cannot change things which go wrong.

- Comprehension: Discuss with students what Greg's mother should do. Should he be punished? How? You may wish to point out that *All's well that ends well* is a **proverb**
- Discuss the meanings of some other well-known proverbs, e.g. *A stitch in time saves nine; Don't judge a book by its cover.*
- Ask your students what title they would give the story.

Speaking and listening: giving directions

Look at the map. It shows the way from Greg's house to Terry's house.

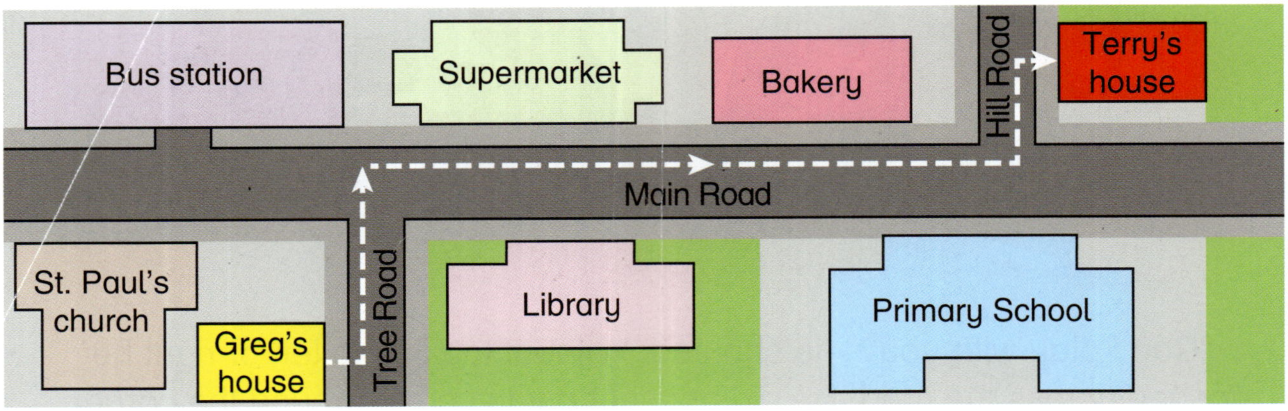

WB 3 p147

1 Put the directions in order.

- 4 Cross the main road carefully.
- 1 Turn left into Tree Road.
- 3 Walk past the supermarket and the bakery.
- 5 Turn left into Hill Road.
- 2 Walk past the library.

2 Give directions from Terry's house to Greg's house. Turn right into Hill Road. Walk past the bakery and supermarket along with the library. Turn right onto Tree Road.

Language: prepositions

Prepositions are words which tell us *where* people or things are.

*Greg went **into** the yard.*

Into tells us where Greg went.

HW 6/05/2021

1 Find seven prepositions in the story below.

Example: 1 across

The cat raced across the road and the dog ran after it. The cat ran into a garden and climbed up a tree. The dog walked around the tree barking loudly. A man shouted at the dog and chased it out of the garden.

- **Speaking and listening:** Prepare for the exercise by working with the whole class to **give directions** to a place in your school, e.g. *from your classroom to the Principal's Office.*
- Students can also use the plan to give directions to different places, e.g. *from Greg's house to the school.*

2 **Complete the sentences with prepositions from the list below.**

WB 3 p63

Example: *Greg walked* past *the library.*

in under through on near across past

1 Greg dashed _________ the road without looking.
2 He lives _________ his friend.
3 The little boy was hiding _________ the table.
4 The children put their books _________ the shelves.
5 Zack walked _________ the market on his way home.
6 The keys were _________ Mom's handbag.

3 **Answer questions about the classroom plan.**

1 Who sits behind Kayla?
2 Who sits next to the window?
3 Who sits between Alyssa and Dwayne?
4 Who sits opposite the door?
5 Who sits next to Rick?
6 Who sits in front of Dwayne?

4 **Write five sentences about your classroom. Use prepositions from the list below.**

behind in front of between next to near opposite

- Exercise 2, Extension: After completing the exercise, some students may be able to make their own sentences using prepositions.

DA Exercise 3: Let students answer in full sentences or answer with one word according to ability.
DA Exercise 4: Allow some students to write two to three sentences.

Word work: prefixes

Prefixes are syllables we put at the beginning of root words to change their meaning.
The prefixes '**un-**', '**im-**' and '**dis-**' mean **not**.

un + happy = *unhappy* (not happy)
dis + obey = *disobey* (not obey)
im + patient = *impatient* (not patient)

WB 3 p77

1 Make new words. Add prefixes from the circle to the words in the box.

Example: un + tidy ➔ untidy

un-
im-
dis-

\+

appear	lucky	approve
patient	like	~~tidy~~
possible	fair	

2 Choose words to complete the sentences.

Example: *My brother says girls cannot play football, but I* disagree.

disobeyed, dishonest, ~~disagree~~, dislike, impossible, unfair, ungrateful, unkind, impatient

1 Greg did not want to wait. He was ________.
2 He did not do what he was told. He ________ his mother.
3 The students did not tell the truth. They were ________.
4 The ________ girl did not thank her aunt for the present.
5 I like helping to cook, but I ________ tidying my room.
6 I help more at home than my sister. I think this is ________.
7 It was ________ to finish all the work in time.
8 Tara was upset because another student was ________ to her.

- Prefixes: Students can learn the spellings of these new words using the tips in Unit 11, page 77.

DA Exercise 2: Allow some students to write answers to fewer questions according to ability.

Writing: write your own story

Write a story about a child who does not do what he or she is told.

1 Getting ideas: Discuss your story.

- Who is the child in your story?
- Why is the child disobedient? What does he or she do?
- What happens in the end?

2 Planning: Copy the story table. Use it to help you plan your story. WB 3 p125

Title of story	
Setting	
Characters	
Plot	Beginning: Middle: End:

3 Drafting: Write the first draft of your story.

4 Revising: Read through your first draft.

Use the checklist below to help you revise it. Then make changes to improve your story.

Checklist for stories

- Have I written clear sentences? ☐
- Does my story have a beginning, middle and end? ☐
- Have I made the story sound interesting? ☐

5 Proofread your story. Correct any mistakes you find. WB 3 p135

6 Write a neat copy of your story.

- **Writing:** Students have practised each stage of the **writing process**, but this is the first time they have put it together. Guide them through the process step by step.
- To help them **revise** their stories, they can read them to a partner and ask for comments. Discuss ways in which they can make their stories more interesting, e.g. using adjectives and synonyms (e.g. *big / huge, small / tiny*).
- Publishing: At the end of the process, students write a neat copy of their work. They do not need to do this every time they write, but you can select different pieces for them to write out neatly.

Looking Back 2

Reading

The Kite Festival

15, Beach Road,
St. John's,
Antigua.
28th March, 2016

Dear Michael,

Thank you for your letter. I hope you are all well in Toronto.

Mommy told me that you are coming to Antigua with Uncle Calvin at Easter. That's great news!

We have our annual kite festival in Antigua at Easter. On Easter Saturday there will be a children's kite-making competition at the Sports Club. We will spend the morning making kites. In the afternoon we will go to the beach to fly our kites. There will be prizes for the best kites. In the evening there will be a family barbecue.

Daddy says he will take us to the competition and help us make our kites. Would you like to come?

- Discuss different reasons for sending letters, e.g. invitations, news, apology, thanks. You may wish to point out the difference between friendly and formal letters.
- **Reading:** As you read, establish the **purpose** for writing the letter and the **audience** (who the letter is written to).

On Easter Monday there will be a kite-flying competition at Devil's Bridge. We will watch the kites from the beach at the end of our road. Last year people came from all over the world to take part. There were more than 500 kites in the sky. Some of them were enormous.

Is kite-flying popular in Canada? What do most people do there at Easter?

Please write back soon and let us know if you would like to take part in the children's kite-making competition.

Your cousin,
Tyrell

1 What relation is Michael to Tyrell?
2 When does the children's kite-making competition take place?
3 Where will the children fly their kites?
4 What will happen on Easter Monday?
5 "*We have our annual kite festival.*" The word *annual* means:
   a) regular **b)** every year **c)** every month
6 Is the kite festival in Antigua a popular event? How do you know that?
7 What is the main reason why Tyrell is writing this letter?
   a) To invite Michael to stay with him.
   b) To invite Michael to a special event.
   c) To tell him how to make a kite.
8 Imagine that you are taking part in a kite-making competition. Describe the kite you would make.

Language

Past tense

1 Complete the sentences with past tense verbs.

Example: *Tyrell* thanked *Michael for his letter.* (thank)

1 Daddy ________ the boys with their kites. (help)
2 Everyone ________ the winner of the competition. (clap)
3 Michael ________ with Tyrell for two weeks. (stay)
4 The wind ________ the kite into the sky. (carry)
5 On Monday they ________ the adult's competition. (watch)
6 Michael ________ to Tyrell's letter the next day. (reply)

- **Reading:** Take the opportunity to revise the layout of a letter.
- **Language:** The first exercise revises the past tense of regular verbs. Before students write answers, provide examples, including verbs with spelling changes (double letters, '-ied').

2 **Retell the story in the past tense.**

made
Tyrell and Michael make kites. They go to the beach. Daddy comes with them. Tyrell sees his friend Danny at the beach. Danny has a kite too. It is a very big kite. The boys try flying their kites. Then Daddy buys them all ice cream.

Owning things

Choose the correct words to complete each sentence.

Example: *Marie lost* her *hat.* (her / hers)

1 The boys are looking for _________ shirts. (their / theirs)
2 The cap belongs to me. It is _________. (me / mine)
3 "Is this _________ bag, Tim?" Mom asked. (your / yours)
4 "These books are _________," the girls said. (our / ours)
5 Anna needs new shoes. _________ are old. (Her / Hers)
6 I bought a new pen. _________ was broken. (My / Mine)

Adjectives

1 **Write the missing words.**

Example: *small* smaller *smallest*

1 cold _________ coldest
2 big _________ _________
3 happy _________ _________
4 beautiful _________ _________

2 **Write sentences comparing one thing to another.**

Example: *The red car is* smaller *than the black car.*

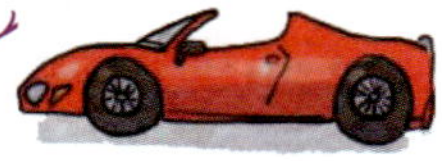

1 a palm tree / tall / a banana tree
2 Tim's writing / tidy / mine
3 a car / expensive / bicycle
4 the weather / hot / today / yesterday
5 sharks / dangerous / dolphins

- Use the exercises on this page to identify the areas which students find difficult. You will find extra practice of these areas in the Workbook.

DA Allow students to write a few sentences from each exercise according to ability.

Word work: word building

1 Divide the words into syllables. Write them in the correct columns.

letter kite barbecue prize festival Easter world popular event enormous flying

One syllable	Two syllables	Three syllables
	lett/er	

2 Which is the root word in these word families?

Example: *helps* *help* *helped* *helpless*

1	painted	painting	painter	paints
2	careful	cared	careless	caring
3	obeyed	disobey	obeys	disobedient
4	colourful	coloured	colouring	colours

Writing: letter of invitation HW 11/3/2021

Write a letter to a friend or family member. Invite him or her to:

Either: a birthday party.

Or: a concert.

1 Plan your letter. Make notes under these headings.

- Name of the event, e.g. school concert
- When the event takes place and where
- What you will do
- Other important information, e.g. what to bring

2 Write the first draft of your letter. Remember to include:

- Your address and today's date.
- The greeting and closing.

Remember!
Don't forget to **sign** your letter at the end.

3 Revise your letter, then proofread it.

Use the checklist on page 59 to help you.

- **Writing:** As a class exercise, produce a list of items to check when students revise their letters, e.g. *Have I used the correct letter format? Have I used full sentences? Do the sentences begin with capital letters? Does the writing 'make sense'?*

Unit 13 Turtles

Get ready

What do you know about turtles?
What would you like to find out about them?

K	W	L
What I **k**now	What I **w**ant to know	What I **l**earned

Reading

The Leatherback Sea Turtle

Leatherback sea turtles have lived in our oceans for 65 million years. They are the largest living turtles. They can be up to two metres long and often weigh more than 300 kilograms. They eat jellyfish and sea plants. They often live more than 40 years.

Where Leatherbacks Live

Leatherbacks spend almost all their life in the sea. However, females always return to the beach where they hatched to lay their eggs. They nest on beaches in the West Indies, in South America and in West Africa.

- **Get ready:** Draw the **KWL chart** on the board. Discuss with students and fill the first two columns with their suggestions. You will complete the third column after reading.
- Pre-reading: Get students to **survey** the text by looking at the layout, photos and headings. Ask: *What kind of text is it (fiction / fact)? What kind of information will you find in it?*

How Leatherbacks Breed

Females come out of the water at night and crawl slowly up the beach. They dig a hole with their flippers and lay about 70 eggs. Then they return to the sea. About 60 days later the young turtles hatch and move quickly towards the water.

Dangers to Leatherbacks

About 25 years ago there were 115,000 female leatherbacks. Now there are only 25,000. Humans are the greatest danger they face. Poachers steal their eggs or kill turtles for their meat. Turtles are often caught in fishing nets. Sometimes people walk on turtle nests by accident and destroy the eggs.

Protecting Leatherbacks

If leatherbacks are not protected, soon there will be none left. On many Caribbean islands there are groups which are taking action. They protect turtle nests, and look after the young turtles carefully until they are old enough to survive in the sea.

1 How big are leatherback turtles?
2 Where do female turtles lay their eggs?
3 How long does it take for the eggs to hatch?
4 In which section of the text can you find information about young turtles?
5 The greatest danger faced by turtles is caused by:
 a) other animals. b) jellyfish. c) people.
6 Why is it important to protect turtles?
7 What is the most interesting thing you learned about turtles?
8 Can you think of any other ways of protecting turtles? What could people do?

- Comprehension: Question 7 should provide information for the 'L' column of the KWL chart. After completing the chart, ask: *What else would you like to know about turtles? Where could you find this information?*

Speaking and listening: finding information

1 Discuss different ways of finding information. Make a list.

Example: looking on the internet

2 Where could you find information about the following things?

- How to make a cake
- Snakes
- Foods which are good for you
- The weather tomorrow
- The name of the Governor General of St. Lucia
- An interesting book for you to read

Language: adverbs

Some **adverbs** tell us **when** or **how often** things happen: *sometimes, often, usually, always, never.*

Female turtles ***usually*** *live in the sea.*

They ***sometimes*** *come out of the sea to lay their eggs.*

WB 3 p38

1 Complete the sentences with suitable adverbs.

sometimes
often
usually
always
never

Example: *Turtles* often *live more than 40 years.*

1 We should ______ steal turtles' eggs.
2 People ______ walk on turtles' nests.
3 I ______ see hummingbirds in my yard.
4 Mongooses ______ kill snakes.
5 People ______ keep a mongoose as a pet.
6 Mongooses ______ live in a pack.

- **Speaking and listening:** Remind students that asking people (e.g. *parents, teachers, librarians*) can be a good way of finding information.
- Adverbs: Adverbs like *sometimes, usually* are **adverbs of time**.

2 **Write your own sentences using the words *sometimes, often, usually, always, never.***

Example: I usually walk to school with my sister.

Some adverbs tell us **how** an action is done.
*The turtles crawl **slowly** up the beach.*
Slowly describes how the turtles crawl.
We add '**ly**' to most adjectives to make adverbs.

3 **Change these adjectives to adverbs.**

Example: *quick* ➔ quickly

quick slow quiet sad loud silent

For adjectives ending in '**l**', we double the 'l'.
careful ➔ *carefully*
For adjectives ending in '**y**', we change the '**y**' to '**i**' and add '**ly**'.
happy ➔ *happily*

4 **Change these adjectives to adverbs.**

noisy greedy helpful angry grateful busy

5 **Complete the sentences with a suitable adverb.**

Example: *A snake moves very* quietly.

1 A snail moves very ________.
2 Lions eat ________.
3 Dogs can run very ________.
4 Ants always work ________.
5 The children shouted ________.
6 I was reading a book ________.

- Adverbs which tell us how actions are done are **adverbs of manner**.
- Exercise 3: Put students in pairs to make sentences using the adverbs they have made, e.g. *Tom can run quickly.*
- Exercise 5: Tell students to use adverbs from this page. Accept '*fast*' as an answer to question 3.

Word work: finding information

You can find a **Table of Contents** at the beginning of a book. It tells you what sections the book contains.

WB 3 p139

1 **Look at the Table of Contents below.**

	Contents	Page
1	Mountains	3
2	Forests	8
3	Oceans	14
4	Animals	20
5	Fish	35
6	Birds	48
7	Insects	60

In which section would you find the answers to these questions?

1 What is the tallest tree in the world?
2 How many oceans are there?
3 Are sharks dangerous?
4 In which countries do parrots live?
5 What do elephants eat?
6 How do bees make honey?

WB 3 p141

An **index** is an alphabetical list of the contents of a book. You can usually find an index at the back of a book.

2 **Study the index. Answer the questions.**

A
alligators 38
anteaters 39
B
bats 52
bees 64
beetles 61
butterflies 70
C
caterpillars 61
crabs 38
D
dogs 24
dolphins 41
E
eagles 50
F
flying fish 35
frogs 28
G
goat 31
goose 55
H
hummingbird 56

- Table of contents: Show students the Table of Contents in this book. Ask questions, e.g. *Which units have poems in them? Where can you find information about water?*
- Index: Show students the skills index at the back of this book as an example.

1 On which pages would you find information about the following?

a) dogs b) geese c) bats d) crabs

2 Where would you look for the answers to these questions?

a) What do butterflies eat?
b) Where do frogs lay their eggs?
c) How do dolphins communicate?
d) Where do anteaters live?

Writing: recording information

1 **Study the information in the table.**

Animal	Size	Habitat	Lifespan	Eats	Important facts
Leatherback turtle	2 m	Ocean	Up to 40 years	jellyfish, sea plants	Need to protect them.

2 **Choose two animals. Find out as much as you can about them. Record the information in a table like the one above.**

3 **Choose ONE of the animals. Write six sentences about it.**

Use the information in your table. Add a picture.

Remember!
After you have written something and revised it, **proofread** it and correct any mistakes you find.

4 **Proofread what you wrote. Use the checklist to help you.**

Checklist for proofreading:

- Do my sentences begin with capital letters and end with **. !** or **?** ☐
- Have I used capital letters for the names of people and places? ☐
- Have I spelt tricky words correctly? ☐

- **Writing:** Draw a table on the board and complete it as a class exercise. Choose an animal students know well, e.g. dog, cat.

DA Some students will find it easier to complete a table about an animal they know well. Others may be able to conduct their own research.

Unit 14 The Three R's

Get ready

What things do you throw away at home?
What things do you throw away at school?

Reading

Caring for the Environment

What we throw away

1 Every day people throw away things they do not need. Paper, plastic and cans take a long time to *decay*. Did you know that it can take 100 years for plastic bags to rot away?

Rates of decay for household waste

What happens to waste?

2 Waste collectors remove *waste* from our homes and take it to dumps outside towns and villages. People throw away so much waste that these dumps are getting bigger and bigger.

- **Reading:** Students **survey** the text as in Unit 13. Ask: *What kind of information does the text contain?*
- They can **predict** the time it takes for everyday items to rot away, then check their predictions.

3 We must reduce the amount of waste we produce. A lot of it will not decay for more than 100 years. Soon, there will not be enough space for it.

4 Sometimes people dump waste in the streets. This creates an eyesore. When the waste begins to rot, it smells bad, and flies *breed* on it. This is dangerous for our health because flies spread disease.

Reduce, Reuse, Recycle

5 We can *recycle* a lot of our waste. Paper can be collected and used to make more paper. We can reuse plastic bags, bottles and glass jars. Fruit and vegetable peelings can be used to make *compost* for our gardens.

Glossary

breed	produce new animals or insects
compost	mixture of decaying plants used to make new plants grow well
decay	rot away naturally
recycle	treat garbage so it can be used again
waste	what is left after we use the valuable part of something

1 Which items decay quickly?
2 Which items take more than 100 years to decay?
3 What happens to the waste we throw away at home?
4 What happens to waste when it begins to rot?
5 An *eyesore* means:
  a) something which can damage our eyes.
  b) something which looks very unpleasant.
  c) something which causes a lot of problems.
6 Which things can we recycle?
7 Why is it important to reduce the amount of waste we produce?
8 How could you reduce waste at school?

- **Glossary:** Get students to work out the meaning of the italicised words by reading them in **context**. They can then use the glossary to check.
- Explain to students what happens when things are recycled.

Paragraphs

A **paragraph** is a group of sentences about a topic. The first sentence usually contains the **main idea** of the paragraph. It tells us what the paragraph is about.

1 Work together to answer the questions.

WB 3 p99

- How many paragraphs are there in the reading text?
- What is the main idea of paragraph 1 in the reading text?

  a) Plastic and paper take a long time to decay.
  b) People throw a lot of things away.
  c) Plastic bags take 100 years to rot away.
- What is the main idea of paragraph 4?

Remember!
The other sentences in the paragraph give **details** about the main idea.

Main idea		Details
Main idea →	We must reduce the amount of waste we produce. A lot of it will not decay for more than 100 years. Soon, there will not be enough space for it.	← Details

2 What is the main idea of paragraph 5? What details are given about the main idea?

Speaking and listening: discuss an issue

1 What kind of waste can be recycled? Make two lists:

- Things we use at home which can be recycled.
- Things we use at school which can be recycled.

2 How do you think we could create less waste?

- **Speaking and listening,** Exercise 1: Give students a few minutes to make their own lists, then brainstorm ideas with the class. Write a class list on the board.
- Exercise 2: Allow students to contribute simple ideas, e.g. *use less paper, don't use plastic bottles.*

Language: conjunctions

We use **and** to join two sentences.
We can collect paper. We can reuse glass jars.
We can collect paper ***and*** *we can reuse glass jars.*
The new sentence has only **one** capital letter and **one** full stop.

1 Join these sentences with *and*.

WB 3 p65

1 Rick picked up the litter. He swept the floor.
2 Grandpa used compost. His vegetables grew well.
3 I picked some tomatoes. We ate them for dinner.
4 On Saturday I tidied my room. I helped Mommy.

We use **and** to add extra information.
I dropped the jar ***and*** *it broke.*
We can also use **but** to join sentences.
I dropped the jar ***but*** *it did not break.*
But tells us something different or surprising.

2 Use *and* or *but* to join these sentences.

Example: Amy fell over but she did not hurt herself.

1 Amy fell over. 2 Mom bought some fruit. 3 We went to the beach. 4 Rick went to the shop. 5 In class we read books. 6 I called my friend.	and but	She did not hurt herself. She put it in her basket. We played cricket. It was closed. We write stories. He did not hear me.

3 Use your own ideas to complete the sentences.

1 On the weekend I ________ and I ___________.
2 I looked for the book but ________________.

- You may wish to tell your students that words like 'and' or 'but' are called conjunctions.
- DA Exercise 2: Give support to some students. Read out each sentence first with 'and' then with 'but'. Discuss which one is correct and why.
- Extension: Students can write more of their own sentences with 'and' and 'but'.

We use **because** to give a reason.
*We should not dump waste **because** it is unhealthy.*

4 **Join the sentences with *because*.**

Example: Mrs. Paul was vexed. There was a lot of paper on the floor.
Mrs. Paul was vexed because there was a lot of paper on the floor.

1 We should not dump plastic bags. They take a long time to decay.
2 We should not cut down forests. We need trees.
3 Grandpa uses compost in his garden. It is good for the plants.
4 Most dumps are very big. People produce a lot of waste.

WB 3 p66 **5** **Match the sentences. Join them with *because*.**

Example: We had a beach clean-up because there was a lot of garbage.

1 We had a beach clean-up.	He felt unwell.
2 Mrs. Paul was pleased.	It was a sunny day.
3 Daddy came home late.	There was a lot of garbage.
4 We went to the beach.	He missed the bus.
5 Dan stayed at home.	The students tidied up.

Commas in lists

We use **commas** between items in lists.
The world has many forests, rivers and oceans.
We do not usually put a comma before **and** in a list.

WB 3 p73 **Write these sentences with commas.**

1 Birds monkeys and snakes live in the forests.
2 We need to protect animals birds and fish.
3 Ants bees and butterflies are insects.
4 We grow tomatoes dasheen yams and sweet potatoes.
5 They sell guava melon apples and pineapple in the market.
6 I ate fried chicken rice and beans for lunch.

DA Allow some students to write the first two or three examples from each exercise according to ability.
- Commas in lists: Students can write lists of more than three items, e.g. things which can be recycled.
- Extension: Some students can make their own sentences with 'and', 'but' and 'because'.

Word work: prefixes

The prefix '**re-**' means 'again'.
re + use = **re**use
*We can **reuse** many of the things we throw away.*

1 **Add the prefix 're-' to these verbs.**

play plant cycle pay write build place

2 **Complete the sentences with the verbs you made.**

WB 3 p78

Example: We can recycle old jars and bottles.

1 After the storm we had to ________ our house.
2 We had to ________ all the broken windows.
3 The students helped to ________ the trees.
4 I had to ________ the exercise neatly.
5 The teams had to ________ the match.
6 You must ________ the money you owe your friend.

Writing: paragraphs

Write a paragraph with the following main idea.

We need to create less waste.

1 **Plan your paragraph. Read the ideas in the box below.**

WB 3 p123

recycle paper make compost reuse plastic bags and bottles
reuse glass jars put recycling bins in classrooms

2 **Write your paragraph.**

- Begin with the main idea above.
- Add details to your paragraph.

You can add your own ideas to the paragraph.

- **Writing:** To help students engage with the task, brainstorm ideas about reducing waste. Compare these with the suggestions in the box above.
- Remind students to revise and proofread their paragraphs.

Unit 15 The Speech

Get ready

Do you help at home? What do your brothers and sisters do? Do you think this is fair?

Reading

The Speech

Last week the students in Akim's class learnt how to give a speech. They practised in pairs. On Monday some of them were ready to talk to the class.

"Who will go first?" asked Mr. Adams.

"We will," said Jade and Shelly.

They stood up in front of the class. "We're going to talk about helping at home," said Jade.

Some of the boys groaned. "Shhhh!" said the girls.

"Women always do more than men," began Jade. "My mother goes out to work, but when she comes home she cooks the dinner and looks after my little sister. My older brother doesn't help. He sits in the chair and reads the newspaper."

"My brother is just the same," Shelly went on. "He never does anything to help. His room is always untidy. In the evening he plays on the computer or watches TV. I have to help Mom to clear the table and wash the dishes. That isn't fair. I like playing on the computer too. We think that everyone should help at home."

- **Reading:** Ask students to **predict** from the picture what is happening in the classroom. Read the title with them and ask students for their opinions on the topic. As you read, compare their **opinions** with those expressed in the speech.

At the end of their speech all the girls clapped loudly.

Akim put up his hand. "I don't think that's fair, sir," he said. "In my home we all help. We take turns to wash the dishes after dinner. If my mother comes home late from work, my father cooks dinner."

Mr. Adams looked at the class. "What do the rest of you think?" he asked.

1 Which jobs does Jade's mother do when she returns from work?
2 What does Shelly's brother do in the evening?
3 Who takes turns to help at home?
4 Why do you think some of the boys *groaned* when Jade started speaking?
5 What does Shelly think is unfair? Why?
6 Which of these are fact? Which are opinion?
   a) Women do more work than men.
   b) Jade's mother goes out to work.
   c) Shelly likes playing on the computer.
   d) Everyone should help at home.
7 Which do you think is better? Why?
   a) Everyone takes turns to do jobs at home.
   b) Everyone has a special task to do each day.
8 Do you agree that women do more work than men? Give reasons for your answer.

Making notes

Notes help us to remember what we want to say in a speech or piece of writing. We can also use notes to record information.

Read the notes Jade and Shelly made for their speech.

WB 3 p128

Subject	Helping at home
Main point	Women do more work than men.
Examples	1 Jade's mom and older brother 2 Shelly's brother
Conclusion	Everyone should help.

- Comprehension: Remind students of the difference between **fact** and **opinion**, as discussed in Unit 11. Encourage students to think beyond the stereotypes expressed by the girls. There may be households where tasks are shared more evenly between males and females.
- Making notes: Explain that notes are a short way of recording information. We do not need to use full sentences in notes. We can also use short forms like 'Mom' and 'Dad'.

Speaking and listening: giving a speech

1 **Choose a topic for a speech.**

Either: Choose one of these topics.

- School uniform
- Homework

Or: Choose a topic of your own.

2 **Prepare your speech.**

- Discuss the topic you chose.
- Make notes about it.
- Practise your speech.

Remember!
Keep your notes. You will need them for the writing task.

3 **Present your speech to another pair of students.**

Ask them to tell you:

- What they liked about your speech.
- How you could make it better.

Language

Contractions

HW 5/31/2021

Contractions are short forms of verbs.

*That **isn't** fair. isn't* = is + not

We put ' in place of the missing letters. We call ' an **apostrophe**.

1 **Find two more contractions in the text on pages 100–101.**

What are the full forms of these verbs? doesn't = does + not
isn't = is + not

- **Speaking and listening:** Explain to students that when they give their opinion in a speech they must provide examples to support it. Point out the examples the girls gave in their speech on pages 100–101.

2 Match the full verbs to the contractions.

Example: *I am* ➔ I'm

I am	it is
it was not	we will
they do not	I can not

we'll	I can't
it's	they don't
I'm	it wasn't

3 Write these sentences in full.

WB 3 p61

Example: *My brother doesn't help.* ➔
My brother does not help.

1 They'll give their speech tomorrow.
2 We don't go to school on Saturdays.
3 It's Jade's birthday tomorrow.
4 I didn't hear what you said.
5 The students weren't ready.
6 We're going to see our friends.

4 Rewrite this note using full verb forms.

Example: It is late.

It's late. I can't wait any longer.
I don't know where you are.
I'm going home now. I hope you're
all right. I'll call you later.

It's is the short form of **it is**.
***It's** sunny today.* ➔ ***It is** sunny today.*

Its shows who or what owns something.
*The bird sat on **its** nest.*

5 Complete the sentences with *it's* or *its*.

1 ________ very hot today.
2 The dog can't find ________ bone.
3 The book has lost ________ cover.
4 ________ your turn now.

- Write examples of contractions on the board before starting the exercises. Explain that we use contractions in speech and in informal writing.

DA Allow some students to write answers to fewer questions according to ability.

Possessive nouns

We use **'s** to show that something belongs to someone.
My brother's room. Shelly's computer.

The girl's T-shirt.

WB 3 p43 **1** **Rewrite using apostrophes.**

Example: 1 the boy's shoes

1 The shoes which belong to the boy.
2 The car which belongs to our teacher.
3 The room which belongs to my brother.
4 The computer which belongs to Mom.
5 The books which belong to Shelly.
6 The food which belongs to the dog.

When the noun is plural or ends in 's', we usually add ' only.
the girls' speech   Mr. Jones' car

WB 3 p44 **2** **Rewrite using apostrophes.**

Example: 1 the girls' games

1 The games which belong to the girls.
2 The book which belongs to James.
3 The bags which belong to the students.
4 The toys which belong to my brothers.
5 The house which belongs to my grandparents.

The boys' T-shirts.

3 **Complete the sentences.**

Example: My brother's room is always untidy. *(brother)*

1 ________ mother works in a bank. (Jade)
2 Our ________ house is near ours. (grandparents)
3 ________ dog is very fierce. (Mr. Evans)
4 I like playing in my ________ garden. (friends)
5 ________ football boots are dirty. (Curtis)

- Explain that for words like 'men', 'women', 'children', we add 's, e.g. *the children's parents*.

DA Allow some students to write answers to fewer questions according to ability.

Word work: opposites

Opposites for you to learn

cheap	expensive
early	late
easy	difficult
first	last
kind	cruel
right	wrong
rough	smooth
safe	dangerous
sweet	sour
true	false

1 Match the opposites.

Example: young – old

~~young~~ open light
laugh quiet night

day dark cry
~~old~~ closed noisy

WB 3 p83

2 Complete the sentences with opposite words.

1 Mangoes are **sweet** but limes are __sour__.
2 My shoes were ________ but my shirt was **dry**.
3 I got to the bus stop **early** but the bus was ________.
4 The first exercise was **easy** but the second exercise was ________.
5 Snails move **slowly** but snakes can move ________.
6 Josh came ________ in the race but Greg was **last**.

Writing: write a speech

1 Write the text of the speech you prepared for the Speaking and listening exercise.
Use the notes you made to help you.

2 Revise your first draft.
Use the checklist to help you.

3 Proofread your speech. Use the checklist on page 59.

Checklist for a speech
- Have I stated my main point clearly? ☐
- Have I given examples to support my main point? ☐
- Are my ideas clear? ☐

- Opposites: Brainstorm opposites students already know before starting the exercises.
- **Writing:** Students can incorporate the feedback they received in the Speaking exercise on page 102.

Unit 16 Grace Goes to School

Get ready

Imagine that another student in your class was ill and could not come to school for a while. What could you do to help this student?

Reading

Grace Goes to School

Look at this picture of my class. That's me in the middle of the front row. I look like everyone else, don't I? I am not the same as the other students. I am disabled.

When I was born, there was something wrong with my spine. This means I can only walk a few steps at a time.

I did not go to school until I was seven years old. My mother taught me at home. In the evenings my brother Kirk and my sister Brianna told me what they had learned at school.

On my seventh birthday, my mother had a surprise for me.

"Your uncle has bought a wheelchair for you, Grace," she said. "When you know how to use it, you can go to school by yourself."

- **Reading:** Get students to **predict** what the story is about from the pictures.
- As they read, ask them to **identify the narrator**. Ask: *Who is telling the story?*

I practised using my wheelchair every day. Soon I was able to wheel myself everywhere.

I was very nervous the first day I went to school. But when Brianna pushed me into the classroom, everyone stood up and cheered.

"Welcome to our class, Grace," said my teacher, Mrs. Davis.

I loved going to school. There was just one problem. When the other students did sports, I had to sit and watch. I longed to run around with them.

Then Kirk had an idea. "Grace can referee our basketball game," he said.

"That's a great idea," said the other students. Now when there are matches, I referee them from my chair.

"We couldn't do without Grace," Mrs. Davis says.

1 Why can Grace only walk a few steps at a time? She has a disabled, wrong

2 How did Kirk and Brianna help their sister? Brianna pushed her into the class and Kirk got her a job on the field.

3 Who bought a wheelchair for Grace? Uncle.

4 A *disabled* person is someone who:

a) has to stay at home.

b) cannot use part of his or her body.

c) is sick all the time.

5 What problem did Grace have at school? She could not play on the field.

6 How was this problem solved? She got to be the referee.

7 Why do you think Grace felt nervous on her first day at school? Because she could not do some stuff.

8 Do you think that Grace will do well at school? Explain your answer. Yes, she may be disabled but she is very smart and kind she can also do most stuff.

- Discuss the 'lesson' of this story with students. Ask: *What did you learn from this story?*
- You may wish to explore attitudes to disability. Give examples of disabled people who have succeeded in life, e.g. blind singer Stevie Wonder or Paralympian Jamol Pilgrim.

Cause and effect

The **cause** is **WHY** something happens.
The **effect** is **WHAT** happens.

CAUSE	EFFECT
Grace cannot walk very far.	She could not go to school.

1 Discuss the cause and effect in these sentences.

WB 3 p97

1 When Grace had a wheelchair she was able to go to school.
2 Grace felt sad because she could not do sports.
3 Grace enjoys sports because she can referee matches.

2 Read these sentences. State what the effect might be.

1 Josh fell over during the football game.
2 Anna did not look before she crossed the road.
3 It rained heavily all night.

Speaking and listening: solving problems

1 Discuss the story. Complete the table.

- What problems did Grace have?
- How were they solved?

Problem	Solution
Grace could not walk very far.	

2 How would you resolve these problems?

- **Speaking and listening,** Exercise 2: After students discuss the two problems, they could describe a problem of their own to their partners and discuss how it could be solved.

Language: quotation marks

When we write, we put **quotation marks** around the words that people say.
"Welcome to our class," *said the teacher.*

1 **Find four examples of quotation marks in the story on pages 106–107.**

2 **Read the conversation. Say the words each person said.**

Example: *How was your first day at school?*

"How was your first day at school?" Mommy asked Grace.
"It was great," Grace said. "All the students cheered me."
"Did you help Grace?" Mommy asked Brianna.
"Yes, I helped her with her sums," Brianna answered.
"Mrs. Davis is very nice," said Grace. "I'm looking forward to going to school tomorrow."

Quotation marks go outside the other punctuation in the speech.
"That's a great idea," said the students.
"Welcome!" said the other students.
"Can I help you?" asked Kim.

3 **Write the sentences using quotation marks.** WB 3 p71

Example: *You can go to school by yourself, Grace's mother told her.*
"You can go to school by yourself," Grace's mother told her.

1 There will be a match tomorrow, Mrs. Davis said.
2 Who will play in the match? the students asked.
3 Kirk scored two points, Grace said.
4 Look out! Daddy shouted.
5 Can we go to the beach tomorrow? the children asked.
6 That's wonderful! they cried.

- Exercise 2: Help students to identify the words which are spoken. Read out the conversation using different words for each speaker.
- Exercise 3: Before students write the exercise, provide practice in using quotation marks. Write direct speech on the board and invite different students to punctuate it.

DA Allow some students to write answers to fewer questions according to ability.

We put a *comma*, an *exclamation mark* or a *question mark* **after** the speech.
"Grace can be our referee," said Kirk.

4 **Rewrite the story. Use quotation marks.**

Remember to put a comma, an exclamation mark or a question mark at the end of the speech.

Example: "Hurry up!" said Mommy.

Hurry up said Mommy.
What time is it asked Anna.
Half past seven said Mommy.
There's plenty of time said Josh.
Here's Daddy with the car said Mommy.
We're ready now Mommy said Josh and Anna.
Bye Bye called Mommy.

Word work: homophones

Some words sound the same but have different meanings and spellings.
***Some** of the students helped Grace with her work.*
*They showed her how to do the **sum**.*

- Exercise 4: Read through the conversation and ask students to identify the speech. Then ask them which punctuation mark should be put at the end of the speech.

Choose the correct words to complete the sentences.

WB 3 p84

1	Brianna waited for her sister. They went home at four o'clock.	(*for* / *four*)
2	Kirk rode his bicycle to school. There was a lot of traffic on the road.	(*road* / *rode*)
3	We are not allowed to eat in class. My teacher asked me to read aloud.	(*aloud* / *allowed*)
4	I waited one hour for my friends. Our friends always help us.	(*our* / *hour*)
5	Do you know the right answer? We had no time to finish the work.	(*know* / *no*)
6	The farmer has a herd of goats. I heard the goats in the yard.	(*heard* / *herd*)

Writing: write your own story

Write your own story about a problem and how it was solved.

Either: Write about something that happened to you or a friend.

Or: Write about an imaginary problem.

WB 3 p124

1 Plan your story. Make notes to help you.

Setting	Names of people in your story. Where and when it took place.
Problem	Describe the problem.
Solution	Explain how the problem was solved.
End	Say how you felt after the problem was solved.

2 Write the first draft of your story.

3 Revise your story. Use the checklist on page 83 to help you.

4 Read your story to another student. Ask this student to tell you:

- what he or she likes about the story.
- how you could make it better.

- **Writing:** Choose one of the problems discussed in the 'Speaking and listening' exercise, e.g. a little brother taking an older child's things. Draw the table on the board and fill it in as a class exercise, using this situation as an example. Encourage students to think about the **effects** of this problem as well as the **solution**.

Unit 17 The Water Cycle

Get ready

How could you find out more about water?
Make up two questions about water. What forms water? Do we drink toilet water but it's cleaned?

Reading

www.waterfacts.com

The Water Cycle

We cannot create or destroy water. The amount of water on the earth today is the same as it was millions of years ago. This is why we need to use water carefully.

The water on earth is recycled. We call this process the **water cycle**. This cycle has different stages.

Stages of the water cycle

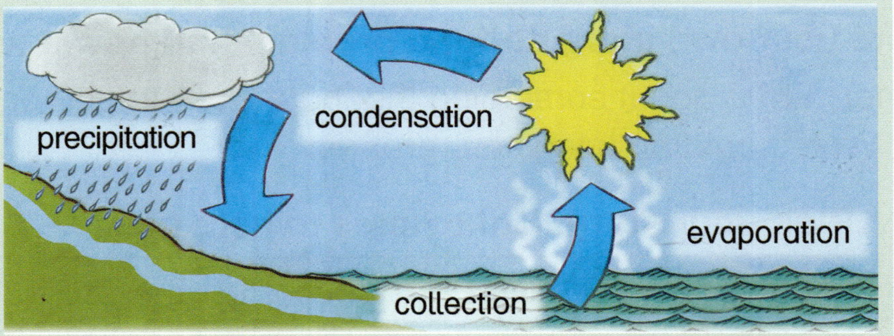

Precipitation

Precipitation happens when there is so much water in the clouds that rain begins to fall. The rain fills our rivers, lakes and oceans. This process is called **collection**. We use the water from lakes and rivers for drinking, washing and watering crops.

Precipitation

- **Get ready:** Encourage students to think of different sources of information to find out about water, e.g. *encyclopaedia, internet, resource persons*.
- **Reading:** Explain difficult words like 'precipitation' to students. Tell them to look at the diagrams and explain in their own words what they can see.

Evaporation

What happens when the sun comes out after it has rained? Steam or vapour rises out of the ground. The steam is known as water vapour. Trees and plants lose water too and add to the vapour. We call this process **evaporation**.

Condensation

As the water vapour rises, it gets colder. It turns into liquid and forms clouds. This is called **condensation**. You can see condensation happening when you pour ice cold water into a glass. Drops form on the outside of the glass. This is because vapour in the warm air turns into water.

Evaporation

What happens after the clouds form? They get heavy and rain starts to fall. The water cycle begins again.

1 Where is rainwater collected? Rainwater is collected from the ocean.
2 What is water vapour? Water vapour is the ground steam.
3 When can you see water vapour rising from the ground?
4 What happens when water vapour rises? When water vapour rises in gets colder.
5 How can you observe the process of condensation?
6 Which of the following statements is true?
   a) We cannot reuse water.
   b) We can use water again and again.
   c) We can create more water.
7 What was the most interesting thing you learned from this internet page? Everything
8 Do you think the internet is a good way of finding out information? Why? Yes because there is mostly true news than fake news on the internet.

- **Reading:** Question 8: Point out to students that not everything on the internet is true They should always check more than one website.
- After reading, ask students if they found the answers to the questions they made in the 'Get ready' exercise. If not, discuss where they might find the answers.

Diagrams and graphs

1 Study the graph. Answer the questions.

WB 3 p151

Annual rainfall in Grenada

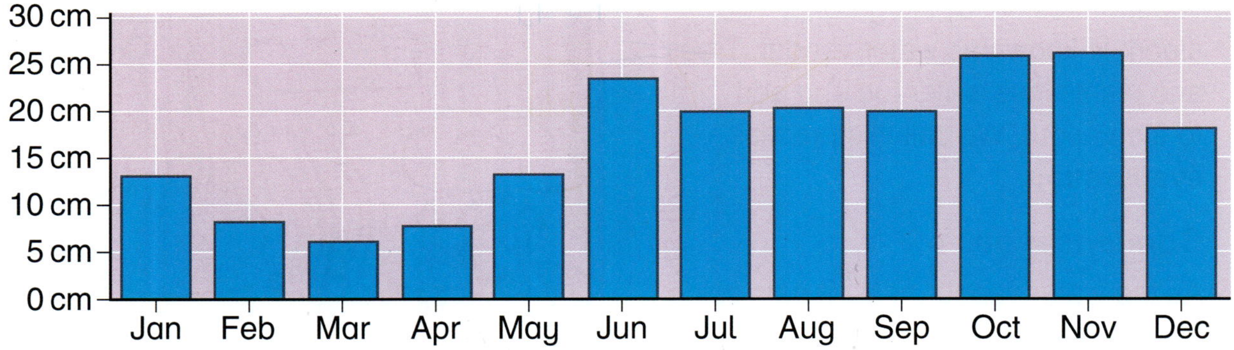

1 Which are the two wettest months in Grenada?
2 Which is the driest month?
3 Which month has more rain, June or July?
4 Which month is drier, January or February?
5 Which months have more than 15 cm of rain each year?

2 Look at the pie chart below. How is water used in Antigua? Make sentences.

WB 3 p150

Example: In Antigua, 20% of water is used for farming.

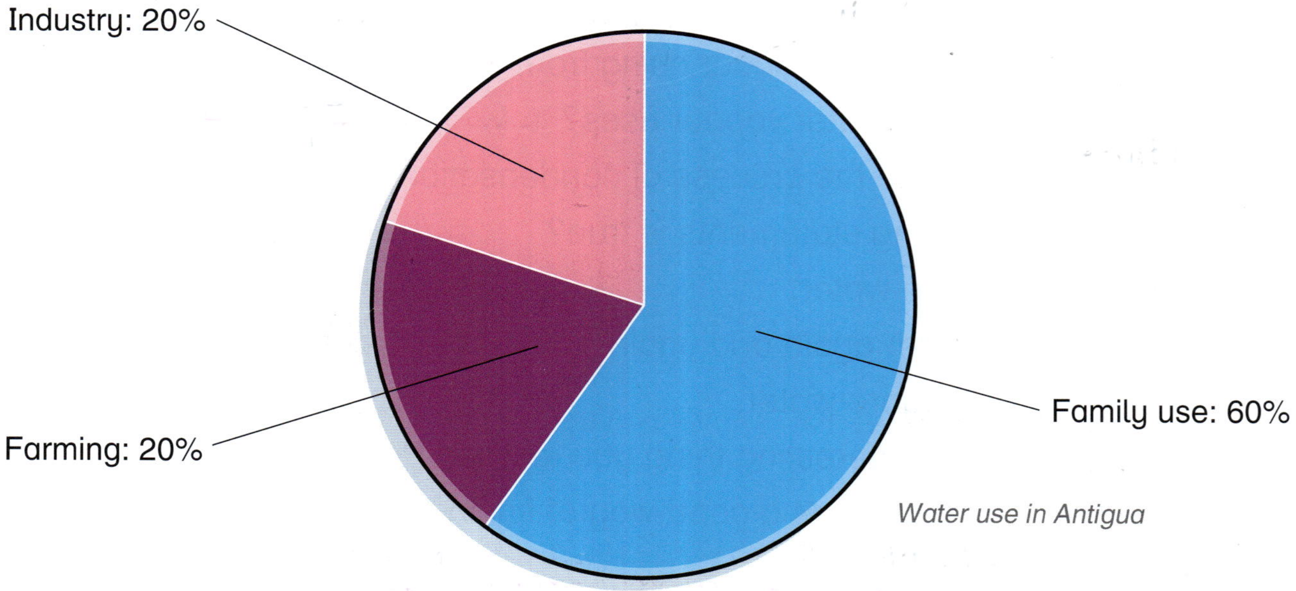

Water use in Antigua

- Exercise 1: Before students attempt to answer the questions for themselves, ask general questions about the graph, e.g. *Which months have the most rainfall? Which have the least rainfall?* Explain that the height of the columns indicates the amount of rainfall for each month.
- Exercise 2: Draw the pie chart on the board and discuss it with students. Ask general questions, e.g. *Which activity uses the most water?*

3 **Read the statements about the pie chart. Are they true or false?**

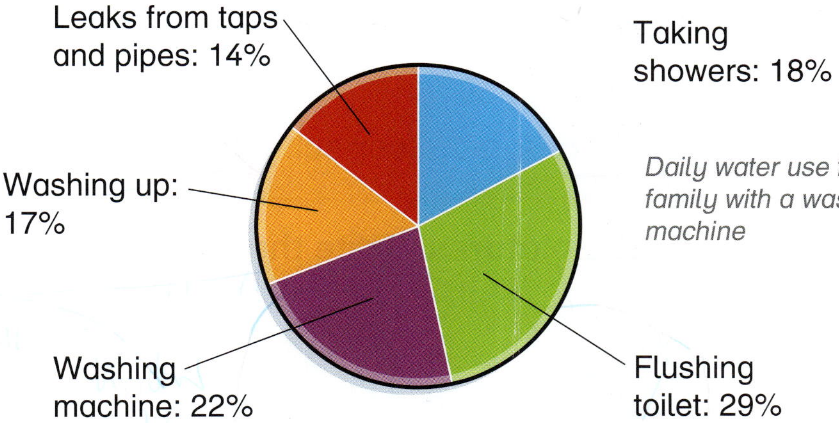

Daily water use for a family with a washing machine

1 Taking showers uses up 18% of the water.
2 Most of the water is lost through leaks from taps and pipes.
3 The family uses more water washing up than taking showers.
4 The washing machine uses 22% of the water.
5 Flushing the toilet uses the most water.

Speaking and listening: discuss information

WB 3 p149

1 **Read the information in the table.**

Activity	Amount of water used
Flushing toilet (*one flush*)	20 l
Shower (*5 minutes*)	100 l
Washing hands (*in basin of water*) Washing hands (*with tap running*)	3 l 8 l
Brushing teeth (*without tap running*) Brushing teeth (*with tap running*)	1 l 10 l
Washing dishes (*in a bowl*) Washing dishes (*with tap running*)	10 l 60 l
Using a washing machine	225 l

2 **Make sentences about the information in the table.**

Examples: Flushing the toilet uses 20 litres of water.
You use less water if you wash your hands in a basin.

- Exercise 3: Explain that the figures in the pie chart represent a 'typical' family. Every family is different however.
- **Speaking and listening:** Ask students to suggest ways in which people could save water.
- Extension: Some students may be able to write sentences about the pie chart and the table.

Language: instructions

We use the **root** form of verbs to give **instructions**.

***Close** the bag. Do not **open** it.*

It is important to give instructions in the correct order.

WB 3 p113 **Match the instructions to the pictures. Write them in the correct order.**

Watch the Water Cycle in Action

You need: a plastic bag, a teaspoon, some water, a rubber band

1. Put two teaspoons of water into a plastic bag.
2. Blow air into the bag. Close it with a rubber band.
3. Place the bag in the sun. Do not open the bag.
4. Look at the bag after half an hour.
5. Note what you see.

Word work: compound nouns

We sometimes put two nouns together to make **compound nouns**.

rain + fall = rainfall *sun + shine = sunshine*

1 **Which two words make each of these compound nouns?**

Example: *bathroom* → bath + room

rainbow	housework
fireman	newspaper
hairbrush	eyebrow

- **Language:** Look at the pictures first. Get students to give instructions. Compare their instructions with the instructions under the pictures.
- Extension: Students can give instructions for another process, e.g. a household activity, or something they have done in a science lesson.

2 **Choose words from each shape to make compound nouns.**

WB 3 p81

Example: *foot + ball* ➔ football

grand super
butter paint ~~foot~~
thunder sea

brush shell
fly father storm
~~ball~~ market

3 **Choose three compound nouns from Exercises 1 and 2. Use each one in a sentence of your own.**

Writing: graphs

1 **Discuss the information in the graph below.**

Annual temperatures in Barbados

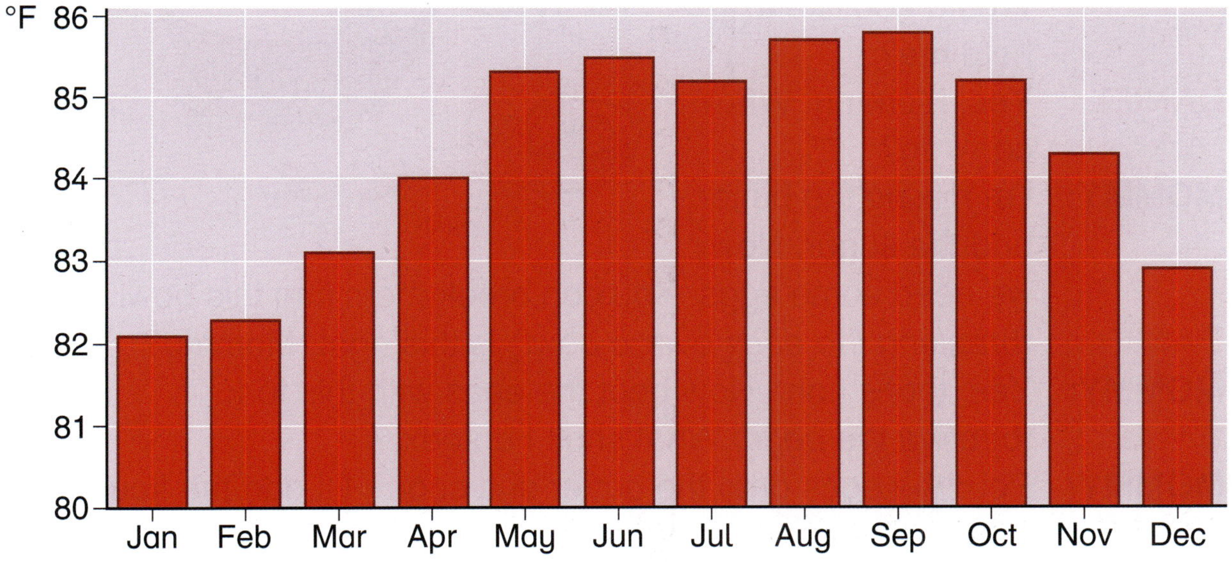

2 **Write a paragraph about temperatures in Barbados.**

Include the following information:

- the hottest months
- the highest temperature
- the coolest months
- the lowest temperature.

3 **Proofread your paragraph and write a neat copy.**

- **Word work,** Extension: Give students words from which they can form their own compound nouns, e.g. *eye (brow / lash), man (sports / fire / police)*.
- **Writing:** Explain to students that the numbers on the vertical axis are °F which means 'degrees in Fahrenheit'. If they are not familiar with this term, tell them that it is a way of measuring temperature.

Unit 18 The Missing Cake

Get ready

Look at the text below. What kind of text is it? How do you know that?

Reading

The Missing Cake

Characters:
DANIEL JOEL KELLIE
MOMMY GRANDMA

Scene 1: the family kitchen, Saturday morning

MOMMY: I'm making a cake for your birthday tomorrow, Daniel. Would you like to help me?

DANIEL: Yes, Mommy. What can I do?

MOMMY: I'm mixing the butter and the sugar. Now we need some eggs. You can break them into this bowl.

DANIEL: (*breaking the eggs over a bowl*) Is this right, Mommy?

MOMMY: Yes, that's right. Now beat the eggs with this fork.

DANIEL: (*beating the eggs*) What shall I do next?

MOMMY: Pour the eggs onto the butter and sugar. I'll add the flour.

DANIEL: When will the cake be ready?

MOMMY: I have to bake it first. We can ice it this evening after Kellie and Joel have gone to bed.

Scene 2: the kitchen, early Sunday morning

KELLIE: Shall we look at Daniel's cake?

JOEL: Good idea! Let's look in the fridge.

- **Get ready:** Talk about the differences between plays and stories. Get students to identify some of the features of a play, e.g. *dialogue*.
- **Reading:** Students use the pictures to predict the events in the play.

KELLIE: *(looking in the fridge)* It isn't in here. Where do you think Mommy has hidden it?

JOEL: Maybe it's in the cupboard. (*looking in the cupboard*) Yes, here it is.

KELLIE: Wow! It looks delicious. I'm going to try a little piece of the icing. Nobody will know. (*She takes the cake out of the cupboard.*)

JOEL: Be careful! You're going to drop it.

(*Kellie slips and drops the cake.*)

JOEL: (*angrily*) Now look what you've done! Mommy will be furious.

(Grandma appears in the doorway.)

GRANDMA: What's going on, children? I heard a noise.

JOEL: We were looking at the cake and Kellie dropped it.

GRANDMA: Oh dear! We can't eat the cake now. It's ruined.

KELLIE: I'm really sorry, Grandma. I didn't mean to drop it.

GRANDMA: (*thinks for a moment*) I have an idea. We won't tell Daniel about the cake right now. We don't want to upset him on his birthday. I'll go to our neighbour's house. She'll help me make another cake. No one will know the difference.

JOEL AND KELLIE: (*together*) Thank you, Grandma.

GRANDMA: Joel, help your sister clear up the mess. Then go back to your room, both of you.

- As you read the play with students, get them to **predict** what will happen next. Discuss the characters' reactions, e.g. *What did you expect Grandma to do when she found the children in the kitchen?*

Scene 3: the kitchen, later the same day

DANIEL: Everything's ready for the party now. I'm going to put the cake on the table. (*going towards the cupboard)*

MOMMY: No, wait a minute, Daniel!

DANIEL: (*opening the cupboard*) Where's the cake?

1 How did Daniel help Mommy?
2 What ingredients did Mommy use to make the cake?
3 When will Mommy and Daniel ice the cake?
4 Why did Kellie and Joel get up early on Sunday morning?
5 Why did Grandma decide not to tell Daniel about the cake?
6 Why do you think that Mommy says "Wait a minute," when Daniel goes to take the cake out of the cupboard?
   a) She knows the cake is not in the cupboard.
   b) She wants to fetch the cake herself.
7 How do you think Daniel felt when he opened the cupboard?
   a) angry **b)** puzzled **c)** excited
8 The play is not finished. What do you think will happen next?

Drama

Look at the way the play is set out:

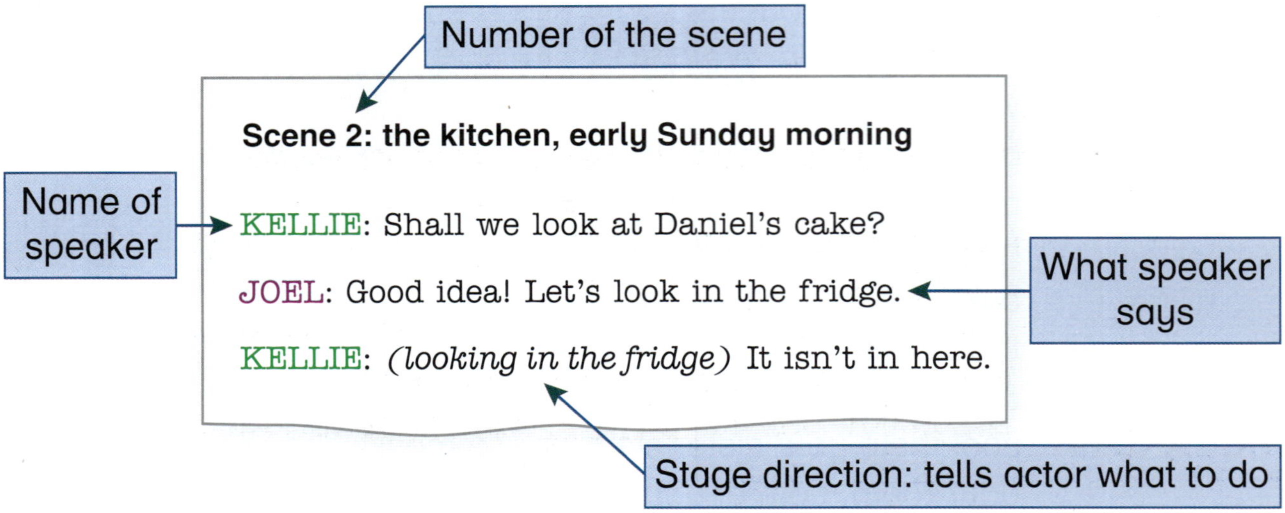

How many scenes are there in the play? Find three more stage directions.

- Comprehension: Ask questions to generate ideas for Question 8, e.g. *Will Grandma bring the cake in time? Will she tell Daniel what happened? Will the party be a success?*
- Drama: Look back at the play and identify the features described above.

Speaking and listening: act a play

Work in groups of five. Act out the first three scenes of the play.

- Discuss how you think the play will end.
- Prepare the ending of the play.
- Act your ending to other groups.

Language: joining sentences

We can use the words ***after***, ***before*** and ***while*** to join sentences.

Mommy iced the cake ***after*** *the children went to bed.*

She baked the cake ***before*** *she iced it.*

Kellie and Joel went into the kitchen ***while*** *Mommy was asleep.*

1 Complete these sentences with *before*, *after* or *while*.

Example: *Mommy iced the cake* before *she put it in the cupboard.*

1 The children cleaned the floor ________ Kellie dropped the cake.
2 Everyone was excited ________ the party started.
3 We played games outside ________ Grandma washed up.
4 We were hot and thirsty ________ we finished playing.
5 Mommy wrapped Daniel's presents ________ he went to bed.
6 Grandpa watched TV ________ Grandma had a rest.

- **Speaking and listening:** Help your students prepare to act out the play. Tell them to decide who will play each part and to think about how they will speak their lines.
- They may want to add more actions and some noises, e.g. *Crash!!!* when Kellie drops the cake.

2 **Complete the sentences. Use your own ideas.**

1 I always feel happy **while** ________________.
2 The students clapped **after** ________________.
3 We practised our play **before** ________________.

We can also join different parts of sentences with ***who*** or ***which***.
Grandma picked up the cake ***which*** *dropped on the floor.*
Your neighbour is the person ***who*** *lives next door.*

WB 3 p45 **3** **Make sentences from the table.**

Example: *After the party Daniel found out* who *dropped the cake.*

1 After the party Daniel found out 2 Everyone liked the cake 3 Grandma went to see the lady 4 Daniel opened the presents 5 A birthday cake has candles 6 A baker is a person	who which	dropped the cake. Grandma baked. lives next door. his friends brought him. you blow out. bakes bread and cakes.

Word work: homographs

Homographs are words which are spelt the same but mean something different.
After the party there was no cake ***left****.*
Daniel uses his ***left*** *hand to write.*

WB 3 p85 **1** **Choose the correct meanings for the words in bold.**

1 A **bat** is used for playing cricket and baseball.
a) sports equipment **b)** small animal

2 Be careful not to **trip** on the step.
a) a journey **b)** fall over

3 Remember to **book** the tickets for the concert.
a) something you read **b)** reserve

4 The huge **wave** almost knocked me over.
a) line of water **b)** hand movement

- Exercise 3: *Who or which?* Explain to students that we use *which* for things and *who* for people.

2 **Give another meaning for each of the following words.**

1 **bark:** a) something which covers tree trunks

b) sound made by a dog

2 **palm:** a) part of your hand

b) ______________________________

3 **light** a) something which is not very heavy

b) ______________________________

4 **pen:** a) place where you keep animals

b) ______________________________

3 **Choose two words from Exercise 2. Make sentences to show their different meanings.**

Example: The bark of the tree is yellow and brown.
The dog gave a loud bark.

Writing: write a scene for a play

Write the last scene for the play on pages 118–119.

Either: Use the ending you prepared for the 'Speaking and listening' exercise.
Or: Use your own ideas.

1 **Write the first draft of your scene.**

2 **Revise your draft. Use the checklist to help you.**

Checklist for writing a play

Have I:

- written the name of each character when he or she speaks? ☐
- written the words each character says? ☐
- included stage directions to tell the actors what to do? ☐

DA Exercises 2 and 3: Allow students to complete these exercises orally according to ability. Some students may be able to write sentences.

- **Writing:** You may wish to complete this as a class exercise first on the board. Let students contribute their own ideas. Encourage them to add extra details when they write for themselves.

Looking Back 3

Reading

Birds of the Caribbean

The Hummingbird

There are more than 300 types of hummingbird and some of them are really tiny. The bee hummingbird weighs only 2 grams. That is less than the weight of two paper clips! Hummingbirds fly so fast that most other birds cannot catch them. They hover over flowers and collect the nectar with their long, slender bills. They are the only bird which can fly backwards. Hummingbirds love to splash in water and take several baths a day.

The St. Vincent Parrot

This parrot is only found on the island of St. Vincent. It is around 40 centimetres long and has mainly green plumage, with blue and yellow tail feathers. Its habitat is in forests on high ground. It eats fruit, nuts and seeds. It makes a loud honking noise when it calls to other parrots. A few years ago there were very few St. Vincent parrots left. It is now a protected species and numbers are increasing.

- Get students to glance at the text and identify the **text type** (factual text). Ask them what **clues** helped them to identify the text type, e.g. headings, photos.

The Bananaquit

The bananaquit is a lively little bird. It is only about 10 centimetres in length. It lives high in trees and makes its nest out of leaves and twigs. Bananaquits pierce the side of hibiscus flowers and suck out the nectar. Some people call the bananaquit the *Sugar Thief*. You can often see one of them stealing sugar from a bowl, or perching on the side of a glass of fruit juice to sip the juice.

Glossary

habitat place where bird or animal lives
hover stay in the same place in the air
nectar sweet juice found in flowers which birds and insects drink
species type of animal or bird

1 Which bird loves sugar?
2 Which bird can fly very fast?
3 Which bird is very noisy?
4 What is special about hummingbirds?
5 Which birds feed on nectar?
6 The St. Vincent parrot has mainly green plumage. *Plumage* means:
a) beak b) feathers c) claws
7 What is the most interesting thing you learned in this reading passage?
8 Which is your favourite bird? Why?

Language

Joining words

Make sentences from the table.

Example: Parrots live in the forest and they eat nuts and seeds.

1 Parrots live in the forest. 2 You can hear parrots easily. 3 We walked in the forest. 4 We went home early. 5 The bird sat on the glass. 6 Mom tried to take a photo.	and because but	They eat nuts and seeds. They make a lot of noise. We did not see any birds. It began to rain. It stole some juice. The bird flew away.

- **Reading:** Encourage students to work out the meanings of unfamiliar words from their context, e.g. *slender, bills, pierce, plumage*.
- You may wish to talk to students about endangered species and the importance of protecting them.

Adverbs

1 Change these words into adverbs.

Example: noisy → noisily

noisy silent
happy careful
fierce hungry polite

2 Choose four of the adverbs you wrote in Exercise 1. Use each one in a sentence of your own.

Example: I heard a blackbird singing noisily.

Quotation marks

Rewrite the sentences using quotation marks.

Example: We sometimes see parrots in the garden, said Dana.
"We sometimes see parrots in the garden," said Dana.

1. What a beautiful bird! said Kim.
2. Hummingbirds can fly very fast, our teacher told us.
3. What is your national bird? asked Josh.
4. Most birds eat fruit, nuts and seeds, said Mrs. Paul.
5. Did you see the parrot? asked Mom.
6. Take care! The path is wet, said the guide.

Apostrophes

Rewrite using apostrophes.

Example: the boys + books → the boys' books

1. Tyrell + letter
2. the birds + nests
3. the twins + mother
4. Mrs. Jones + car
5. my sister + toys
6. the children + kites
7. the bird + beak
8. James + father

- Adverbs: Revise the spelling changes needed when 'ly' is added to adjectives.

DA Quotation marks: Give some students support by writing the sentences on the board. Choose students to underline the words which are spoken.

Word work: opposites

Complete the sentences with opposite words to the words in bold.

Example: *It was noisy in the town but in the forest it was* **quiet**.

1 The gardens are ________ on Saturday but on Sunday they are **closed**.
2 Kim's bag was **light** but mine was ________.
3 Bats sleep during the **day**, but fly around at ________.
4 Josh had ________ shoes but his T-shirt was **old**.
5 The pineapple was **expensive** but the bananas were ________.
6 The glasses are **clean** but the plates are ________.

Writing: record information and write a paragraph

1 **Study the fact sheet below.**

Facts about birds

Name of bird: St. Vincent parrot
Habitat: forests on high ground
Size: 40 cm long
Diet: fruit, nuts and seeds
Interesting fact: It makes a loud honking noise.

2 **Make a fact sheet about *either* the bananaquit *or* the hummingbird.**

3 **Choose a bird or animal you know well. Prepare a fact sheet about it.**

Find out more about this bird.

- **Either:** Look in an encyclopaedia.
- **Or:** Look it up on the internet.

4 **Write a paragraph about the bird or animal you chose.**

5 **Proofread your paragraph. Correct any mistakes you find.**

- **Writing:** Choose a bird or animal and write a fact sheet on the board as a class exercise. Remind students how to **proofread** their writing. Write on the board a list of points to check.

DA Some students may find it easier to write about an animal they know well.

The Writing Process

Generating ideas
Choosing a topic, getting ideas, organising ideas, planning

Students can get ideas from:
- drawing a picture
- talking to a partner
- class discussion
- creating a word web.

They can organise their ideas:
- in the order in which things happen
- by sorting their ideas into groups.

↓

Writing a first draft
Putting ideas into sentences

Students can:
- write captions for a drawing
- work with a partner of different ability
- write independently.

Praise students for their efforts. Don't expect 'correct' writing from early writers.

↓

Revising
Making it more interesting

Ask students to:
- re-read their writing
- read their writing to a partner
- ask themselves.
  - Are the ideas clear?
  - Can I make it more interesting with adjectives or different verbs?

↓

Proofreading
Checking punctuation and spelling

Ask students to:
- re-read looking just for one thing, e.g. full stops or capital letters.
- read again looking for something else, e.g. the spelling of tricky words.

↓

Publishing
Making a neat copy for others to read

Rewriting is hard work for students of all abilities.
- Select occasional pieces of writing for display or to put in a class book.
- Explain why you would like them to make a neat copy (*purpose*) and who is going to read it (*audience*).

It is important to demonstrate to beginner writers *how* people write.
'Think aloud' as you model the stages on the board. Involve students in drafting, revising and proofreading. Focus on one of these per session.

Sample Compositions

Sample story

Question: Write a story about a child who was naughty.

Story title	Kitten in the Tree
Characters	Grandma, Ricardo, Tanice, Daddy, the kitten
Setting	Tanice's garden
Beginning	Tanice has kitten for birthday
Middle	Ricardo chases kitten up tree Kitten won't come down
End	Tanice has idea Kitten comes down

Kitten in the Tree

Tanice always wanted to have a pet. When she was eight, Grandma gave her a sweet little kitten for her birthday. *(Characters and setting)*

Tanice loved the kitten. She often played with it in the garden.

Tanice's brother, Ricardo, liked playing tricks. One day he chased the kitten up a tree. *(Beginning)*

The kitten was scared. It did not want to come down. Tanice stood under the tree. She called the kitten, but it climbed further up the tree.

The children called Daddy. He got a ladder and put it against the tree. He climbed up the ladder, but he could not catch the kitten. *(Middle)*

Then Tanice had an idea. She fetched a bowl of milk and put it under the tree. The kitten loved milk. It jumped onto Daddy's shoulder, and Daddy climbed down the ladder with it.

Soon the kitten was drinking the milk greedily. Tanice sat and watched it, but Ricardo was hiding. *(End)*

- Read the story with students and discuss how the characters and setting are introduced at the beginning.
- Follow the order of events in the middle part of the story. Ask students to predict how the kitten will come down from the tree.
- Point out that at the end of the story, the writer keeps readers guessing. *Why do they think that Ricardo is hiding?*

Sample Letter

Question: You recently went to stay with your aunt and cousins. Write a letter to thank your aunt for your visit.

Address

PO Box 215,
Roseau,
Dominica.

Date

15th September, 2016

Greeting

Dear Auntie Carla,

I hope you are well. Mommy and Dana send you their best wishes.

Reason for writing

Thank you very much for having me to stay. I really enjoyed my visit.

Body of letter

I loved going to Fort Shirley and seeing the old buildings. I told Mommy and Dana about the time we went swimming, and had a beach picnic. I think we were really lucky to see dolphins.

Writer's news

We went back to school yesterday. I have a new teacher this year. She is very nice.

Questions

How are Jason and Leah? Do they like their new school? I hope they can come and stay with us during the Christmas holidays.

Closing

Your niece,

Signature

Marie

- Point out the five parts of the letter: address, date, body, closing and signature.
- Talk about the information in the letter and identify the main idea of each paragraph: (1). Opening remarks (2). Purpose of letter (3). Talking about the visit (4).The writer's own news (5). Questions to the person receiving the letter.

Sample expository text

Question: Write about an animal or bird which is common in your country.

Planning

Animal	Opossum (Manicou)
Size	Same as small cat
Lives	2–4 years
Appearance	Grey fur, black ears and eyes, pink nose, feet, tail Sharp teeth
Characteristics	Shy, not fierce
Habitat	Forests
Diet	Insects, snails, berries, fruit
Interesting facts	Sleep in daytime, hunt at night Use tail to help them climb trees Females carry babies in pouch for 2–3 months

Opossums

Opossums are found in several Caribbean islands. Some people call them manicous. They are the same size as a small cat and they live for two to four years. ← Introduction

Opossums have grey fur with black ears and eyes, and pink noses, feet and tails. Opossums have very sharp teeth, but they are not fierce animals. They are quite shy. ← Appearance, characteristics

Opossums often live in forests. They use their long tails to help them climb trees. They sleep in the daytime and hunt at night. They eat insects and snails. They also eat fruit, leaves and berries. ← Habitat, diet

Female opossums carry their babies in a pouch on the front of their bodies. The babies stay in their mother's pouch until they are two to three months old. ← Opossums and their babies

- Remind students that they need to conduct research when they prepare to write an expository text. The notes at the top are the result of research into opossums.
- Help students to see how the information is organised in paragraphs. Discuss the main idea of each paragraph.

Sample description

Question: Describe a place where you like to be.

Planning

My bedroom

What room looks like
window, pale blue walls, pictures

What I do there
open window, hear sounds, read, draw

Things in room
bed, table for books and pencils

How I feel there
happy, do what I want there

My bedroom is quite big. It has a window facing the sea. Last year, Daddy painted my bedroom pale blue. I have pictures of my favourite animals and flowers on the walls. ← What room looks like

My bed is in the corner under the window. I sleep there every night. Beside my bed there is a table where I keep my books and my pencils. ← Things in room

When I wake up in the morning I open the window and look out. I love to feel the cool breeze on my face. Sometimes if it is windy, I can hear the waves crashing on the beach.

On the weekend I do not go to school. In the morning I stay in my room and read or draw. Often I can hear Mommy and Daddy talking in the kitchen. Sometimes I can smell Mommy making toast. ← What writer does there

I love my bedroom. It is my favourite place because I can do what I want there. ← How writer feels and why

- Show students how the writer uses a concept map to plan the description.
- Discuss which senses the writer uses in the description, e.g. colour of room – *sight*, sound of waves – *hearing*, toast – *smell*, cool breeze – *touch*. Explain that we do not need to include all five senses in a description. We can focus on one or two senses. Here, the writer focuses mainly on the senses of sight and hearing.

Sample book review

Question: Write a review of a book or story you read recently. Say what you liked about it and why.

Planning

Title	The Anansi Stories
Characters and setting	Anansi, Tiger, Snake The forest, a long time ago
Plot	Anansi gets the stories for himself
Best part	Tiger gives stories to Anansi
Why I liked it	Anansi was very clever

The Anansi Stories

This story is about Anansi and Tiger. It takes place in the forest a long time ago.

Anansi is jealous of Tiger because the stories the animals tell are called the Tiger Stories. Anansi wants the stories for himself. Tiger promises that Anansi can have the stories if he brings Snake to him alive.

Anansi plays a trick on Snake and ties him to a bamboo branch. Tiger is very surprised when the little spider brings him Snake, but he keeps his promise.

The best part of the story is when Tiger gives the stories to Anansi. Tiger did not expect Anansi to bring him Snake alive.

I liked the story because Anansi is very clever. He is much smaller than Snake, but he gets him to do what he wants.

Title

Characters, setting

Plot

Best part

Why I liked story

- Discuss why people write book reviews, e.g. *to get other people to read the books*.
- Point out that book reviews are written in the present tense. Emphasise that students do not need to retell the whole story.
- Students can keep their book reviews in a reading journal.

DA Some students can write notes, as in the example at the top of the page, according to ability.

Glossary

Adjective	Word used to describe a noun or a pronoun, e.g. *a* **big** *house, it was* **big**.
Adverb	Word used to describe how something is done, e.g. *The girl ran* **quickly**.
Alliteration	Repetition of the same sound at the beginning of words that are close, e.g. **T***ropical* **T***aste.*
Antonym	Word with the opposite meaning to another word, e.g. *tall/short.*
Apostrophe	Punctuation mark used to show ownership, e.g. *the boy's books, the students' classroom.*
Conjunction	Words used to join sentences and parts of sentences, e.g. *and, but, because.*
Contraction	The short form of verbs and their subjects, e.g. I will → *I'll*, I cannot → *I can't.*
Homograph	Word which is spelt the same as another word but has a different meaning, e.g. **palm***: part of hand, kind of tree.*
Homophone	Word with the same sound but with different spelling and meaning, e.g. **week:** *period of 7 days,* **weak:** *not very strong.*
Noun	Word which refers to a person, animal, thing or place, e.g. *Jason, girl, dog, chair, river.*
Onomatopoeia	Word which imitates a sound, e.g. *splash, bang.*
Paragraph	Group of sentences about a main idea.
Phrase	Group of words which usually do not make complete sense on its own, e.g. *the weather on Sunday, going to the beach.*
Predicate	Part of a sentence which contains the verb, e.g. *The children* **loved to play on the beach**.
Prefix	Letters added to the beginning of a word to change its meaning, e.g. *pay* → **re***pay, happy* → **un***happy.*
Preposition	Word which shows position and time, e.g. **on** *the table,* **at** *midday.*
Pronoun	Short words used to replace nouns, e.g. *they, them, mine, yours.*
Quotation marks	Punctuation mark used to show words which are spoken, e.g. *"I like this book," said Tyler.*
Root word	The main part of a word to which other syllables can be added, e.g. **paint** → *painting, painter, painted.*
Simile	Phrase which compares one thing to another, e.g. *The stars* **were like diamonds**.
Subject	Person, place or thing which does what the verb describes, e.g. **The boy** *kicked the ball.*
Suffix	Letter or group of letters added to the end of a word to make a different word, e.g. *colour* → *colour***ful**.
Syllable	Word or part of a word with one vowel sound, e.g. *boy* (one syllable), *stu/dent* (two syllables), *ba/na/na* (three syllables).
Synonym	Word with similar meaning to another word, e.g. *afraid / scared.*

Skills Index